THE J. PAUL GETTY MUSEUM

· HANDBOOK ·

OF THE COLLECTIONS

THE J. PAUL GETTY MUSEUM

· HANDBOOK ·

OF THE COLLECTIONS

THE J. PAUL GETTY MUSEUM
MALIBU · CALIFORNIA
1988

Published 1986. Second edition 1988.
© 1986, 1988 The J. Paul Getty Museum
17985 Pacific Coast Highway
Malibu, California 90265

Mailing address:
P.O. Box 2112
Santa Monica, California 90406

(213) 459-7611 administrative offices
(213) 458-2003 parking reservations

Sandra Knudsen Morgan, managing editor
Andrea P.A. Belloli, manuscript editor
Patrick Dooley, designer
Karen Schmidt, production coordinator
Kathe Flynn and Kurt Hauser, production assistants
Elizabeth C. Burke, photograph coordinator
Donald Hull, Stephenie Blakemore, Thomas Paul Moon,
    Penelope Potter, Jack Ross and Charles Passela,
    photographers

Typography by Andresen Typographics, Los Angeles
Printed by Nissha Printing Co., Ltd., Kyoto, Japan
Library of Congress Cataloging-in-Publication Data

J. Paul Getty Museum.
    The J. Paul Getty Museum handbook of the collections.

    1. Art—California—Malibu—Catalogs. 2. J. Paul
Getty Museum—Catalogs. I. Morgan, Sandra Knudsen.
II. Title.
N582.M25A627   1985   708.194'93   85-23121
ISBN 0-89236-084-4 (pbk.)
ISBN 0-89236-087-9 (hbk.)

CONTENTS

FOREWORD

"If a museum is alive and thriving, it is bound to keep changing and improving. This is good for our visitors and good for our staff. But it means that guidebooks go quickly out of date." Thus wrote my predecessor, Stephen Garrett, just four years ago in a guidebook that obeyed his rule and went quickly out of date. We are pleased to present its successor but cheerfully resigned to the new *Handbook*'s speedy obsolescence.

The Getty Museum's collection now grows at such a rate that the galleries need to be rearranged frequently, and a room-by-room commentary would be a short-lived thing. This *Handbook* is not a guide, therefore, but a selection of important works from the collection with some interpretive remarks by the curators. By way of introduction we provide a concise account of Mr. Getty's life as a collector and of the Museum's brief but remarkable history. Later in 1986 we also plan to publish a book that treats the building—its design, construction, and historical precedents—in greater detail than the old guidebooks or other Museum publications.

It has been ten years since the present Museum building was opened to the public. The building has weathered gently, the bright colors of the painted decorations in Roman style have softened, and the trees and shrubs have grown up. Public perceptions have changed as well, since trends in contemporary architecture have made the re-creation of a Roman villa a less outlandish notion than it may have appeared in 1974. Inside the Museum the changes are more striking, for the galleries display a great many newly acquired works of art. Only attentive readers of newspapers and magazines, however, are likely to know how profoundly the Getty Museum has changed in the decade since the villa opened.

Mr. Getty's generous legacy gave the trustees a chance to undertake much more than the improvement of the Getty Museum, which in any event could never absorb all the income. In 1983 they formed the J. Paul Getty Trust, a private operating foundation (as distinct from a grantmaking foundation) devoted to the visual arts. After two years of consultations with professionals in museums, universities, and

View of the Main Peristyle Garden and main facade, The J. Paul Getty Museum, 1980. Photo: Julius Shulman.

schools here and abroad, the officers of the Trust defined a program to employ Mr. Getty's endowment for the maximum public benefit. The primary goals of the Trust's programs, in addition to the continued growth of the J. Paul Getty Museum, are the advancement of the study of the history of art and related disciplines; the improvement of the documentation of art and of tools for scholarly research; the strengthening of the study, practice, and documentation of art conservation; and the fostering of wider and better education in the arts in American schools. The Trust's current activities are recounted in some detail in the essay that follows on Mr. Getty's art collecting.

The J. Paul Getty Museum now has opportunities for expansion and improvement that could never have been imagined when it opened in 1974. Important new works of art have been acquired in the areas of the Museum's three traditional interests: antiquities, French furniture and decorative arts, and European paintings. Classical antiquities, especially Greek and Roman sculpture, comprise the largest of the Museum's collections. There is also an important group of Greek vases and much fine Etruscan, Greek, and Roman terracotta and bronze work. Mr. Getty had a particular passion for the exquisitely made French furniture and decorative objects of the eighteenth century. Old master paintings include several dozen examples of very great importance, among them a group of fine seventeenth-century Dutch paintings. There are also Italian, French, and Spanish paintings of great distinction and a small but growing group of nineteenth-century pictures.

Entire new collections have been formed as well and four new curatorial departments created. The Museum has bought drawings gradually and selectively since 1981; there are already about a hundred examples of remarkably high quality. The collection now ranks among the finest for its size in the world. In 1983 the Museum entered the field of illuminated manuscripts with the purchase of the most important group of Medieval and Renaissance manuscripts then in private hands. In 1984 it was possible to seize another exceptional opportunity and acquire a number of the best private holdings of photographs in the world. Together they now form the finest museum collection of photographs in this country. All of the drawings, manuscripts, and photographs are now available for study by students and scholars, and a selection of each group is on public view in changing exhibitions. The Museum is also acquiring sculpture and works of art from European countries other than France, the collection's traditional focus. Important statues of the sixteenth through the nineteenth centuries have begun to make their way into the galleries. Maiolica and glass have been added through several major acquisitions of private collections.

The Museum aims to build a collection of modest scope but considerable distinction. It will not become a large, general collection but will remain relatively specialized, and our traditional emphasis on publication and conservation will be maintained. A new Getty Museum building—together with facilities for other activities of the Trust, including the Getty Center for the History of Art and the Humanities and the Getty Conservation Institute—will be built on a recently acquired 742-acre property in the foothills of the Santa Monica Mountains. The new museum building, to be designed by architect Richard Meier, will house the collections from the Middle Ages through the nineteenth century, while the building in Malibu will be renovated to serve as America's only museum devoted to Greek and Roman art.

We hope our visitors will not only enjoy the pleasures of the collection and its setting but will also share some of our exhilaration at the opportunities the Museum has in its future.

John Walsh, Jr.
Director

Figure 1. Yousuf Karsh, Canadian, b. 1908. J. Paul Getty, *1964.* ©*1964, Yousuf Karsh.*

J. PAUL GETTY AND HIS MUSEUM

J. Paul Getty combined the lives of oil-field wildcatter, shrewd and spectacularly successful businessman, writer, and member of the international art world. His attitude toward art and collecting was complex. Although he maintained that "fine art is the finest investment," he also felt that "few human activities provide an individual with a greater sense of personal gratification than the assembling of a collection of art objects that appeal to him and that he feels have a true and lasting beauty." Mr. Getty frequently voiced admiration for the ideal of the Renaissance man, who pursues knowledge, beauty, and truth for their own sakes. As a vigorous citizen of the modern world, however, Mr. Getty also advocated harnessing these ideals to those of achievement, progress, and the attainment of excellence.

When he died on June 6, 1976, at the age of eighty-three, Mr. Getty had collected art for over forty-five years. It was not uncommon for him to abandon a meeting with oil company associates in order to talk late into the night with collectors, dealers, or art historians about his museum, about the artist Raphael—a particular passion—or about a new purchase. He was not an obsessive collector like William Randolph Hearst or Joseph Hirshhorn, but collecting was a part of his life that he relished and about which he felt very deeply. In later years he sometimes called himself an addict who could not stop himself from buying works of art. He frequently wrote about the joys of collecting, as in an essay published in 1965:

> I am convinced that the true collector does not acquire objects of art for himself alone. His is no selfish drive or desire to have and hold a painting, a sculpture, or a fine example of antique furniture so that only he may see and enjoy it. Appreciating the beauty of the object, he is willing and even eager to have others share his pleasure. It is, of course, for this reason that so many collectors loan their finest pieces to museums or establish museums of their own where the items they have painstakingly collected may be viewed by the general public.

J. Paul Getty was born in 1892 in Minneapolis, Minnesota. He was known during his adult life as Paul. His father, George F. Getty, was a successful attorney and already wealthy when he entered the oil business in Oklahoma in 1903. The elder Getty moved his family to southern California in 1906. An only child, young Paul loved to read and enjoyed such sports as swimming and boxing. His father planned to have him enter the

*Figure 2. Gerald Brockhurst, English, b. 1890. J. Paul Getty, 1938. Oil on canvas,
73.5 x 61 cm (29 x 24 in.). 67.PA.2.*

family business and encouraged him from the age of sixteen to work
summers in the Oklahoma oil fields.

In 1909, after graduating from high school, Paul Getty made his first
visit to Europe with his mother and father. He remembered that as part of
the tour they visited the Louvre and the National Gallery in London;
later he admitted that neither had made much of an impression on him at
the time. After a semester at the University of Southern California and
three terms at the University of California, Berkeley, he made a trip to
China and Japan in May–June 1912, returning with a few pieces of carved
ivory, bronzes, and lacquer work—a foretaste of his later passion for
collecting. In November 1912 Mr. Getty returned to Europe as a student

at Oxford University to read political science and economics, with a view to entering the diplomatic service. He received his diploma in June 1913 and set off on a *Wanderjahr*. In later years Mr. Getty described his young self as a model tourist, faithfully making the rounds of the museums and galleries from Sweden and Russia to Greece and Egypt, but he could recall being impressed by only one painting, the *Venus* by Titian in the Uffizi.

After spending the tense early days of World War I in London with his parents, Mr. Getty began a trial year of joint ventures in the Oklahoma oil fields with his father. In 1916 he brought in his first producing oil well, qualifying at age twenty-three as a millionaire. Mr. Getty was proud of his success in the rough-and-tumble life of the oil fields and almost fifty years after felt that he was still a wildcatter at heart.

The roaring excitement of the Oklahoma boom towns may have had an attraction for the quiet and persistent young man, but he returned to Los Angeles in July 1916 and announced to his startled parents that he was ready to retire. When the United States entered World War I, he applied to the United States Army Air Service, was not called, and spent a couple of years savoring the pleasures of being young and rich in California. Parental expectations and the thrill of his own business ventures, however, gradually led him into a pattern of living about seven months of the year in Europe and five months in the United States.

When his father died in May 1930, Mr. Getty became president of George F. Getty Incorporated, the family oil firm; after this he frequently declared that he "no longer had any freedom of choice over what I would do with the rest of my life." His interest in the oil industry never slackened, and indeed it provided his chief occupation until the day he died.

Perhaps as a relief from his business responsibilities, Mr. Getty found his interest in art developing. He read voraciously on the subject and visited museums whenever he could. He later claimed that—paradoxically—the more his appreciation and love of fine art grew in the mid- and late 1920's, the more his knowledge dampened any inclination to collect, since very few works of art of good quality were for sale at that time. The United States and Europe were enjoying a period of tremendous prosperity, and great numbers of wealthy collectors—including Hearst, the Mellons, and the Rothschilds—bid against each other enthusiastically for whatever came on the market. Mr. Getty also felt strongly that he needed to reinvest most of his profits in his expanding business enterprises. When this situation changed with the panic of 1929 and the Depression, the time seemed right to begin collecting works of art. Of this period Mr. Getty wrote:

> I would not have thought of purchasing antiques had prices been
> at their former level. I learned that a collapse in the price of
> antiques had commenced in 1930, and that objects of high quality

*Figure 3. Joaquin Sorolla y Bastida,
Spanish, 1863–1923.* The Wounded
Foot, *1909. Oil on canvas, 109 x 99 cm
(42¹⁵/₁₆ x 39 in.). 78.PA.68.*

could be purchased in 1937 for a fraction of their market value in
the first thirty years of the twentieth century. I asked myself why
this should be so and if it were likely to continue long in the
future. Fine art objects are limited in number, and the originals can
never be replaced. I thought that the comparatively low prices
afforded an opportunity to acquire for investment a small but
select art collection.

In March 1931 Mr. Getty purchased his first art object of value, a
landscape by the seventeenth-century Dutch artist Jan van Goyen, at
auction in Berlin for about $1,100. This isolated purchase was followed
two years later, in November 1933, by the acquisition at auction in New
York of a group of ten paintings by the Spanish Impressionist Joaquin
Sorolla y Bastida, whom Mr. Getty admired for his brilliant treatment of
sunlight. *The Wounded Foot* (fig. 3) has remained a favorite with visitors to
the Malibu museum.

Mr. Getty often said that he was inspired to collect the decorative arts
after leasing a penthouse in 1936 from Mrs. Frederick Guest on Sutton
Place South in New York. The apartment was furnished with French and
English eighteenth-century pieces to whose charm Mr. Getty responded
enthusiastically. In later years he was frequently asked why he devoted so
much of his energy to acquiring carpets, tapestries, and furniture and not
the paintings and sculpture that are more prominent in the great art collections of the twentieth century. He claimed that there were two reasons:

> First, I do not subscribe to the theory that only paintings, sculp-
> ture, ceramics, and architecture qualify as major fine arts. To my
> way of thinking, a rug or carpet or a piece of furniture can be as
> beautiful, possess as much artistic merit, and reflect as much
> creative genius as a painting or a statue. Second, I firmly believe
> that beautiful paintings or sculptures should be displayed in
> surroundings of equal quality. Few men would dream of wearing

Figure 4. Bernard Molitor, French, 1730–ca. 1815. Roll-Top Desk, ca. 1790. Mahogany veneer; gilt bronze mounts, 136.5 x 177.8 x 86.3 cm (53¾ x 70 x 34 in.). 67.DA.69.

a fifty-cent necktie with a three-hundred-dollar suit, yet all too many collectors are apparently content to have their first-rate paintings hang in a room with tenth-rate furniture that stands on a floor covered with a cheap machine-loomed carpet.

A period of intense buying began in June 1938, when Mr. Getty purchased many of the major pieces of French eighteenth-century furniture offered at the Mortimer Schiff sale in London. Fear of impending war inhibited bidding, and prices were far below what had been anticipated. Bidding for himself, Mr. Getty acquired at one stroke the beginnings of a significant collection. In later years he said, "My collection like Gaul can be divided into three parts: before Schiff, Schiff, and after Schiff." Among the purchases were a magnificent Savonnerie carpet, the famous roll-top desk by Bernard Molitor (fig. 4), a side table with Sèvres plaques by Martin Carlin, a damask sofa and chairs by Jean-Baptiste Tilliard *fils* (see p. 174), and two Chinese porcelain vases with French gilt bronze mounts.

The purchase that may have given him the most pride was the Ardabil Carpet (fig. 5), a large Persian carpet made during the first half of the sixteenth century to adorn the most holy of all the Persian religious shrines, the mosque of Safi-ud-din. The beauty of this carpet was so prized that the Persians held it "too good for Christian eyes to gaze upon." The Ardabil and its three lesser companion carpets disappeared from the mosque early in the nineteenth century. One entered the

Figure 5. Ardabil Carpet. Persian, Safavid dynasty, ca. 1540. Wool and silk, 729 x 409 cm (23 ft. 11 in. x 13 ft. 5 in.). Los Angeles County Museum of Art 53.30.2.

Figure 6. Attributed to Raphael (Raffaello Sanzio), Italian, 1483–1520. The Holy Family, ca. 1509. Oil on panel, 120.5 x 91 cm (47⁷/₁₆ x 35¹³/₁₆ in.). 71.PB.16.

Figure 7. Rembrandt van Rijn, Dutch, 1606–1669. Portrait of Marten Looten, 1632. Oil on panel, 92.7 x 76.2 cm (36¹/₂ x 30 in.). Los Angeles County Museum of Art 53.50.3.

collections of the Victoria and Albert Museum, London, in 1893. The others subsequently made their way into the hands of the art dealer Lord Duveen. When Mr. Getty first saw the Ardabil Carpet on loan from Duveen to an exhibition of Persian art in Paris in 1938, he declared it to be one of the most beautiful things he had ever seen. His attempts to acquire it immediately were frustrated, as Duveen wished to keep it for his own private collection. However, in the summer of 1938, Mr. Getty's persistence and the fear of war persuaded Duveen to sell him not only the Ardabil Carpet but also one of the two small prayer rugs from the same mosque.

In succeeding months Mr. Getty bought a large number of paintings, the beginning of the Museum's present collection. A purchase that fascinated him for the rest of his life as an example of the high drama of collecting was made at an auction at Sotheby's on July 20, 1938. Lot number 49, the *Holy Family*, then known as the *Madonna of Loreto* (fig. 6), was catalogued as "after Raphael." Seeking advice, Mr. Getty turned to Gerald Brockhurst, the fashionable English portraitist who had painted him that same year (fig. 2). Brockhurst told Mr. Getty that the foreshortening of the Virgin's right arm betrayed Raphael's own touch. Mr. Getty bid cautiously for himself and got the painting for £40, roughly $200. This bargain painting remained a favorite and inspired his longlasting fascination with Raphael. In 1963 Mr. Getty had the painting cleaned, after which art historian Alfred Scharf declared it to be Raphael's lost original. Mr. Getty subsequently loaned the *Holy Family* to the National Gallery, London, for several years. (Further research and the cleaning of a second version of the Raphael in the Musée Condé, Chantilly,

Figure 8. Pier G. Vangelli, Italian,
J. Paul Getty, 1939. Marble, H: 53.25 cm
(21 in.). 78.SA.40.

Figure 9. Portrait Bust of the Empress Sabina.
Roman, ca. A.D. 135. Marble, H: 43 cm
(10⅞ in.). 70.AA.100.

have recently shown that the Getty painting is a good contemporary
workshop copy.)

The acquisition of Rembrandt's *Portrait of Marten Looten* (fig. 7) was
equally controversial, although for a very different reason. Mr. Getty
bought the painting, executed by Rembrandt in 1632 when he was
twenty-six, at the sale of the Anton W. W. Mensing collection. Mr. Getty
had been attracted by the painting when it was on display in the Museum
Boymans-van Beuningen, Rotterdam, and bid for it anonymously at the
sale in 1938. When his bid was successful, there was an outcry in the
Netherlands about losing a national treasure to an "unnamed American."
Still anonymously, Getty loaned the portrait for exhibit in the Fine Arts
Pavilion of the 1939 New York World's Fair, thus enabling him "to share
his joy in owning the masterpiece with millions of people."

During the summer of 1939 Mr. Getty was in Rome, where he sat for
a marble portrait bust by Pier Vangelli (fig. 8), who introduced him to
the Vatican workshops, where the American visitor was especially fascinated by the mosaics. He spent much time looking at ancient Roman
monuments and seriously considered purchasing the magnificent Nilotic
mosaic at Palestrina, which then belonged to Prince Barberini. While Mr.
Getty did not acquire the mosaic, he did buy two Roman portraits of the
empresses Livia and Sabina (fig. 9), after seeking advice from Ludwig
Curtius, then director of the Deutsches Archäologisches Institut. Mr.
Getty's friendship with Curtius lasted until the latter's death. With
characteristic enthusiasm the new purchases also were loaned to the
New York World's Fair in 1939.

World War II completely curtailed Mr. Getty's activity as a collector.

Figure 10. J. Paul Getty at Jerash, early 1950's.

He threw most of his energies during the war years into expanding and running Spartan Aircraft Corporation in Tulsa, manufacturing aircraft and training pilots. One of his slogans for the war effort characterizes his attitude toward all things: "You did fine yesterday, but what have you done today? You have to sell yourself to me every day."

Immediately following the war, Mr. Getty remained in the United States, converting Spartan to peacetime production. But by 1947 he was back in Europe, living in hotel rooms and negotiating deals with the burgeoning European oil market and for the development of oil fields in North Africa and Arabia. Development of a fully integrated worldwide oil network—producing, transporting, refining, and marketing—soon made Mr. Getty's company a strong competitor to the giant Seven Sisters of the oil world. Despite the global reach of his operations, however, he always described himself as "a small fellow who ran a one-man show."

Mr. Getty's major avocation continued to be centered around art. He visited museums, archaeological sites (fig. 10), and art dealers, and carefully recorded in his diary works of art that impressed him (and often their prices). On a memorable visit to Delphi in 1952, he saw the famous bronze charioteer and noted with the true collector's passion, "If I owned this statue, I don't believe I would trade it for any work of art in the world." He always compared his pieces with the ones he admired; he also listened to experts and carefully recorded their views.

By the early 1950's Mr. Getty again had begun to add to his collections, partly in order to furnish his several houses. In 1945 he had acquired a sixty-five-acre citrus ranch in a valley on the Pacific Coast in

Figure 11. Lansdowne Herakles. Roman, ca. A.D. 135. Marble, H: 193.5 cm (76³/₁₆ in.). 70.AA.109.

Los Angeles as a retreat for himself and his last wife, Theodora (Teddy) Lynch. The longer he remained abroad, the more difficult it became to extricate himself from the European center of his businesses, especially as a personal aversion to travel grew. In 1951 Mr. Getty left on his regular summer trip to Europe and never returned to the United States.

At this time Mr. Getty began to donate works of art from his collection to various museums for tax purposes. Recipients included the Santa Barbara Museum of Art, Oberlin College, and the San Diego Museum of Art. The most dramatic gift was in 1953, when he gave the Los Angeles County Museum of Art two of his most prized possessions, the Rembrandt *Portrait of Marten Looten* and the Ardabil Carpet; the gift also included other carpets and tapestries. Writing later, Mr. Getty said he felt that the carpet was too "good" for his private use and that therefore he had decided to donate it. Later in 1953, colleagues, notably Norris Bramlett, persuaded him to consider establishing a museum in his own name. The ranch house in Los Angeles seemed an ideal location.

The trust indenture executed by Mr. Getty in late 1953 remains the only document in which he specified how his money was to be used. In that indenture he authorized the creation of a "museum, gallery of art and library" and stated the purpose of the trust very simply as "the diffusion of artistic and general knowledge." It seems likely that at this time he envisioned his ranch museum on a more personal and modest scale than that of the public museum in Los Angeles.

It was in the early fifties that Mr. Getty made his first important purchases of antiquities. In rapid succession he bought the life-size marble Lansdowne Herakles (fig. 11; see p. 34), three sculptures from the Earl of Elgin's collection at Broom Hall (including the Elgin Kore [see p. 28]), and the fifth-century–B.C. Cottenham Relief. His collection gained significance almost overnight. Greek and Roman sculpture was to be a continuing passion, for Mr. Getty appreciated it as the most enduring record of the beauty of the human form.

The Herakles remained a personal favorite until the end of Mr. Getty's life. The myths of the virtuous and beneficent demigod had a definite appeal for the American philanthropist, as did the sculpture's connections with the Roman emperor Hadrian, in the ruins of whose villa it had been found, and with a noble British collection. Mr. Getty wrote with considerable delight about the history of the Lansdowne Herakles, which was probably a second-century–A.D. Roman work based on Greek prototypes developed during the fourth century B.C. Two years after being restored in Rome, the statue was purchased by the Marquess of Lansdowne, remaining in Lansdowne House in London and at the family's country seat of Bowood for more than a century. There it was praised by such authorities as Adolf Michaelis as

Figure 12. Funerary Stele of Myttion. Greek, ca. 390 B.C. Pentelic marble, 71 x 24 cm (28 x 9⁷⁄₁₆ in.). 78.AA.57.

"perhaps the most important classical statue in English collections." It was assumed that the family could never be induced to part with it or, at the very least, only for an astronomical price. They had not sold an antique sculpture since 1930, when John D. Rockefeller, Jr. successfully had bid £28,000 (then nearly $140,000) for the *Wounded Amazon*, now in the Metropolitan Museum of Art, New York. However, to Mr. Getty's incredulous joy, the family decided to sell him the Herakles for £6,000.

Mr. Getty was also particularly interested in French furniture. In 1949 he even published a short book entitled *Europe in the Eighteenth Century,* a distillation of his own studies of European culture and history. In a long chapter on French decorative arts, the illustrations are almost entirely of furniture in his own collection. One of his most notable purchases was made soon after, in 1952: the famous double desk by Bernard van Risenburgh that had belonged to the dukes of Argyll since the late

Figure 13. Titian, Italian, 1477–1576, and his workshop. The Penitent Magdalen, *1530. Oil on canvas, 106 x 91.4 cm (41³⁄₄ x 36 in.). 56.PA.1.*

eighteenth century (see p. 160). Mr. Getty was both rueful and amused that he had missed an opportunity to inspect the desk at Inverary Castle, where—a year before—it had been sold to a dealer. Presumably he felt he could have bought it for less.

The J. Paul Getty Museum was opened to the public in May 1954 for two afternoons a week (Wednesdays and Saturdays) and by reservation for groups on other days. Although Mr. Getty continued to buy works of art for his private residences, the best pieces began to appear in the Museum, which also acquired a small staff. The distinguished art historian Wilhelm R. Valentiner, who had been director of the Detroit Institute of Arts and, most recently, of the Los Angeles County Museum of Art, was made director in 1954. He remained for two years. However, neither Dr. Valentiner nor his curator, Paul Wescher, exerted much influence on Mr. Getty's acquisitions. George F. Getty II, Mr. Getty's eldest son, became director shortly after Dr. Valentiner and remained until his death in 1973. Mr. Getty himself then served as director until he died.

In the mid-fifties Mr. Getty tried to build all three of his collections—paintings, decorative arts, and antiquities—with some consistency. During this period he met the famous connoisseur Bernard Berenson and passed much time talking with him and studying art in the library at Villa I Tatti in Settignano, not far from Florence. Photographs of some of Mr. Getty's recent acquisitions were shown to Berenson, who especially admired a young girl's funerary stele inscribed with her name, Myttion, from the fourth century B.C. (fig. 12).

Under Berenson's influence, Mr. Getty began to take an increasing interest in Italian Renaissance painting and to acquire Italian pictures to add to the Dutch and English paintings he already owned. He continued to believe, however, that in architecture, sculpture, and literature the ancients surpassed the achievements of the Renaissance. Although the sums he spent on paintings were often greater than those spent on antiquities and decorative arts, Mr. Getty generally got less for his money when buying pictures, as he was well aware. His feelings on art and the art market at this time are expressed in *Collector's Choice,* an unusual book he wrote with Ethel LeVane in 1955. There he summarizes his approach to collecting: "I buy the things I like—and I like the things I buy—the true collector's guiding philosophy." In a conversation recorded in the book, Mr. Getty is asked: "Why did you specialize in collecting eighteenth-century French tapestries and furniture, seventeenth-century Savonneries, and sixteenth-century Persian carpets rather than paintings, which are the choice of most collectors?" He responds:

Figure 14. J. Paul Getty on the cover of TIME *magazine, February 24, 1958.*

> Partly for that very reason. I never like to follow the crowd....A good painting is fine to look at—or to own. But pictures have become too fashionable. People will pay a hundred thousand dollars for a second-rate painting by a second-rate master and believe they're getting value....In classical statuary, French furniture, tapestries, and carpets I consider I have...masterpieces. Yet if paintings were my preference, I could never hope to compete with the Louvre, the Prado, or fifty other fine collections.

Mr. Getty enjoyed research and endeavored to study his acquisitions thoroughly, often employing scholars to help him ascertain the aesthetic values, provenances, and former prices of works of art under consideration. Comfortable in six languages—English, French, Spanish, German, Italian, and Latin—and slightly familiar with Greek, Arabic, and Russian, Mr. Getty had an approach to research that was both wide-ranging and individual. He frequently lamented that he lacked sufficient leisure to follow up all the clues.

In some ways Mr. Getty saw himself in the tradition of other great and eclectic collectors, such as his own older contemporary William Randolph Hearst or the Roman emperor Hadrian. In his diary Mr. Getty compared the architecture and investments represented by Hadrian's Villa and Hearst Castle at San Simeon with his own holdings in art and real estate. He was gratified to own works of art that great connoisseurs of the past had owned and cherished. He was hesitant, however, about his paintings collection, which he evidently expanded mostly in order to broaden his new museum's appeal to visitors. He bought some Impressionist canvases and Italian primitives, and—in an attempt to replace the *Marten Looten* with another star—bought the *Penitent Magdalen* by Titian in 1956 (fig. 13). Although it has since become apparent that the painting is only one of seven versions of the composition and is not well preserved, at the time it had a good scholarly reputation and a high price.

In October 1957 an article in *Fortune* magazine listed Mr. Getty, until then a virtually unknown businessman, as the richest American. A cover portrait from *Time* in February 1958 shows him reserved and hardly joyful about his new fame (fig. 14). From then on the American public began to use the Getty name as a synonym for wealth. Mr. Getty was uncomfortable about the attention paid his personal fortune and attempted to deflect it into discussions of the number of jobs his corporations created through reinvestment of profits. Also in 1957 a gallery was added to the small ranch museum in Los Angeles, and all of the recent antiquities and decorative arts purchases were installed (figs. 15, 16). Then Mr. Getty abruptly informed Paul Wescher by cable: "I think the JPG museum has enough pictures. We have no space for any more." This resolution was kept for almost a decade.

Much of Mr. Getty's interest for the period between 1958 and 1968 was centered on Sutton Place, a manor house built twenty-five miles southwest of London in 1521-1526 by one of Henry VIII's courtiers. The house was acquired in 1959 by a subsidiary of the Getty Oil Company both as the parent company's new international headquarters and as Mr. Getty's personal residence (figs. 17, 18). He was fascinated with the history of his beautiful home and could recite the chronicle of the manor of Sutton year by year. He was proud of the fidelity with which the architecture and furnishings had been restored to the eclectic elegance of an English country house.

Mr. Getty continued to acquire art through a subsidiary corporation, Art Properties, Inc. One major acquisition, made in 1961, was *Diana and Her Nymphs Departing for the Hunt* (fig. 19), attributed to Rubens, which hung in the Great Hall at Sutton Place (fig. 18) until it was given to the Museum in 1971. Another was the Rembrandt portrait of a man with a knife, now identified as *Saint Bartholomew* (see p. 97), in 1962. Both acquisitions were notable for the high prices Mr. Getty was now willing to pay for paintings he liked, although later that year he was appalled by the amount ($2.3 million) the Metropolitan Museum of Art paid for Rembrandt's *Aristotle Contemplating the Bust of Homer*, which started a new era of high prices.

In the 1960's and early 1970's, Mr. Getty felt compelled to examine his motives as a collector and as the richest man in America. One consequence was the biography *J. Paul Getty: The Richest American* by Ralph Hewins, published in 1961. Another was an increase in Mr. Getty's charitable contributions, mostly to the university his parents had attended (Ohio Northern); the Smithsonian Institution, Washington, D.C.; the World Wildlife Fund; and his own Museum, where Anne Jones was now curator. At the same time he asked several of his scholarly friends to help him describe the results of his first thirty years of collecting. Jean Charbonneaux, curator at the Louvre; Julius S. Held, professor at Barnard College, Columbia University; and Pierre Verlet,

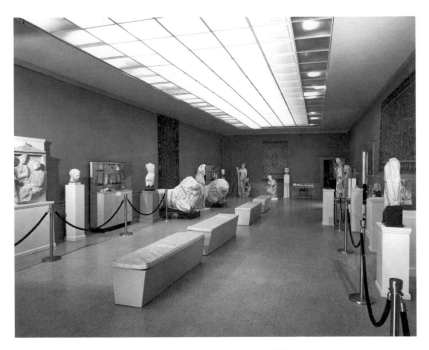

Figure 15. Antiquities gallery, The J. Paul Getty Museum, ca. 1965.

Figure 16. Decorative arts gallery, The J. Paul Getty Museum, ca. 1965.

Figure 17. The yew alley, Sutton Place, 1959. Photo: Julius Shulman.

Figure 18. J. Paul Getty being interviewed by Intertel in the Great Hall, Sutton Place, 1959. Photo: Julius Shulman.

Figure 19. Attributed to Peter Paul Rubens, Flemish, 1577–1640. Diana and Her Nymphs Departing for the Hunt, *1615/18. Oil on canvas, 235 x 182.9 cm (92¹/₂ x 72 in.). 71.DA.14.*

curator of furniture and objets d'art at the Louvre, helped him write *The Joys of Collecting*, published in 1965. The three scholars attempted to point out both the strength and individuality of the collection. Mr. Getty's own introductory essay summarizes his "addiction" to collecting art and details some of the highlights of his career as a collector. It describes vividly "the romance and zest—the excitement, suspense, thrills, and triumphs—that make art collecting one of the most exhilarating and satisfying of all human endeavors."

In 1964 Mr. Getty bought the full-length *Portrait of a Man* by Veronese (see p. 90) that was subsequently loaned to the National Gallery, London. By 1967 he had resumed buying at auctions. His interest in his Museum also revived, and in the coming years he donated large sums for the purchase of works of art, most notably the *Portrait of Agostino Pallavicini* by Anthony van Dyck (see p. 105). The Museum now had a new curator, Burton B. Fredericksen, who, with other advisers, especially Federico Zeri, recommended objects to Mr. Getty for purchase.

During 1968 Mr. Getty decided to expand his Museum. At first he intended only to add a new wing to the home to which he still expected to return. Gradually, however, he evolved the idea of a major art museum that he could leave as a gift to the people of Los Angeles. He could have donated his collection to any of dozens of cities around the world, giving to the host city the responsibility for constructing a building, maintaining a museum, and raising operating expenses. But, as he wrote,

> ...there were other, and for me, overriding considerations. It was my intent that the collections should be completely open to the public, free of all charges—be they for admission or even for parking automobiles. Nothing of this sort could be insured if the museum were under the control of a city, state—or even the Federal—government.

To this end he eventually invested more than $17 million in a new building and endowed the Museum to meet payroll and operating expenses. He wished to make sure that his gift to the people of California was complete and free of future operating expenses.

In 1968, however, Mr. Getty had not yet decided what kind of museum to build. He had only one stipulation in his initial instructions to the Museum's trustees: "I refuse to pay for one of those concrete-bunker type structures that are the fad among museum architects—nor for some tinted-glass and stainless-steel monstrosity." Various alternatives were proposed: Spanish Colonial style to suit the existing ranch building, Neoclassical to suit the Greek and Roman sculpture collection.

Then—quite unexpectedly—one evening at Sutton Place Mr. Getty announced to a group of guests that he wished to build a separate large building on the ranch site and that it might be an accurate re-creation of the Villa dei Papiri in Herculaneum. Some quick research in the Sutton Place library revealed that the villa had been one of the largest ever built in the ancient Roman empire and had possibly been owned by Lucius Calpurnius Piso, father-in-law of Julius Caesar and patron of the Epicurean philosopher Philodemus. The villa had stood outside the walls of Herculaneum on the Bay of Naples and had been destroyed and buried along with that city and Pompeii when Mount Vesuvius erupted in A.D. 79. Mr. Getty eagerly reviewed the scanty information about the villa's architecture, the considerable number of sculptures it housed, and the papyrus scrolls retrieved from it through tunnel excavations in the middle of the eighteenth century. He wanted a museum building that would itself be a work of art or of historical interest, and the decision to re-create the Villa dei Papiri must be seen in this light.

Throughout his life, of course, Mr. Getty had been fascinated by ancient Greece and Rome, and he had two houses in Italy, one near Ostia and one near Naples. The best explanation for his choice of architectural prototype is still in his own words:

> The public should know that what they will finally see wasn't done on a mere whim or chosen by a committee delegated for such a task. It will simply be what I felt a good museum should be, and it will have the character of a building that I would like to visit myself...the principal reason concerns the collection of Greek and Roman art which the museum has managed to acquire...and what could be more logical than to display it in a classical building where it might originally have been seen? There is, I believe, no other place in the world where one can see such a building in any state except ruins, as one sees them now in Pompeii. There are replicas and imitations of ancient public buildings but none of a private structure—so this one should provide a unique experience.

In any event the project was a challenge. Mr. Getty wanted the re-creation to be as faithful as possible, but the only records of the villa were

Figure 20. Aerial view of the J. Paul Getty Museum, 1980. Photo: Les Nakashima.

Figure 21. View of the Main Peristyle Garden, The J. Paul Getty Museum, 1980. Photo: Julius Shulman.

sketchy notes and plans made by the Swiss engineer Karl Weber in the eighteenth century. The Museum building also had to be efficient as a structure in which Mr. Getty's art collection could be displayed and enjoyed by the public. It had to include such twentieth-century requirements as elevators, restrooms, and security systems at the same time that the public areas, both indoors and out, had to be permeated by an appropriately Roman feeling. The site was a narrow valley in Malibu, a few hundred yards from the Pacific Ocean, and the structure had to pass the stringent Los Angeles municipal building codes.

A team of consultants and other personnel was assembled. Stephen Garrett, the architectural consultant, made a total of seventeen trips between Malibu and Sutton Place acting as Mr. Getty's eyes and ears. Dr. Norman Neuerburg was the historical consultant who advised on everything from construction techniques and materials to parallels for every feature of Roman domestic architecture, from ceiling vaults and grillwork to wall and floor decoration. It was he who found solutions that would be acceptable to scholar, contractor, and building inspector alike. Emmet Wemple and Denis L. Kurtz designed the gardens, creating with sight and scent the illusion of an ancient Roman setting. Langdon and Wilson were the Los Angeles architects, and Dinwiddie Construction Co. was general contractor. Ground was broken in December 1970, and three intense years of work produced the results that delight three hundred thousand visitors a year (figs. 20, 21). Sadly enough, Mr. Getty never saw his new museum.

During construction, which started in mid-1971, Mr. Getty and the trustees realized that the new building would provide an enormous increase in gallery space. From 1970 to 1974, a large number of works of art was purchased, and the professional staff was enlarged. In 1971 Gillian Wilson was hired as curator of decorative arts. Bernard Ashmole advised on antiquities purchases, and in 1973 Jiří Frel became curator of antiquities. Buying reached a peak in 1971 and 1972, culminating in the purchase at auction of the famous *Death of Actaeon* by Titian—which, however, the Museum was not permitted to export from England and which now belongs to the National Gallery, London.

The new J. Paul Getty Museum building opened its doors to the public in January 1974. Greek and Roman art set the tone because of the architecture and gardens and also because the entire main floor was devoted to antiquities. It was generally recognized that this part of the collection was of very great importance—perhaps ranking third in America after the massive holdings of the Metropolitan Museum of Art and the Museum of Fine Arts, Boston—despite significant gaps, particularly in the area of original Greek art. Relative to other museums, however, the French furniture was the finest of the three Getty collections, with paintings remaining the least developed. Acquisitions continued to be made at a lesser rate in all three areas between January 1974 and June 1976, the month of Mr. Getty's death, but after four years of intensive buying, it was time to shift the Museum's emphasis to assimilation, research, and catalogue preparation.

At his death, Mr. Getty bequeathed a vast legacy to his Museum, leaving it to the trustees' discretion to decide how it should best be used. In the first years after he died, the collections grew significantly through the receipt of Mr. Getty's private collection and some purchases made under then-director Stephen Garrett and with the guidance of Otto Wittmann; in 1979 the latter became a trustee and adviser as well as chairman of the Acquisitions Committee. Significant purchases included the fourth—third-century-B.C. Greek bronze Victorious Athlete attributed to a follower of Lysippos, for which Mr. Getty had negotiated for several years; the *Saint Andrew* by Masaccio; and the corner cupboard by Jacques Dubois (see pp. 42, 87, and 163).

Recently the scope of acquisition has expanded to include objects outside Mr. Getty's three original collections: old master drawings, illuminated manuscripts, European sculpture and works of art, and photographs. Under the directorship of John Walsh, appointed in 1983, the Museum intends to strengthen and broaden the collections and further improve public services. Eventually the entire collection except for antiquities will move to a new building to be designed by architect Richard Meier on a 742-acre site in the Brentwood area of West Los

Angeles. The present building will then be entirely devoted to Greek and Roman art, appropriately housed in the re-created Roman villa.

By April 1982, with the receipt of the proceeds of Mr. Getty's estate, the J. Paul Getty Trust already had begun to prepare for its transformation from a small museum into a visual arts institution of international significance. The terms of Mr. Getty's bequest established that the Trust would not be a grant-making foundation but rather an operating foundation that creates and administers its own programs. Harold M. Williams, who had been appointed president and chief executive officer the previous May, led a small staff in an initial year of exploration to determine where in the fields of art and art history the Trust's resources and energies might best be focused. The objective was to identify a series of activities that would make a significant contribution to the visual arts and related areas of the humanities. Discussions were held with a broad range of art historians, museum curators and directors, educators, conservators, and other knowledgeable professionals in the United States and abroad. Small groups of experts also were convened to discuss specific needs and priorities. A responsive and supportive relationship with other institutions in the field was a major goal.

Since May 1982 the trustees have made commitments to six operating activities in addition to the further growth of the Getty Museum. These activities are the Getty Center for the History of Art and the Humanities, the Getty Conservation Institute, the Getty Art History Information Program, the Getty Center for Education in the Arts, the Museum Management Institute, and the Program for Art on Film, a joint venture with the Metropolitan Museum of Art. Staff and facilities for the first two of these programs will be housed, together with the new Museum building, at the West Los Angeles site in Brentwood; construction should be finished in the early 1990's. It is hoped that the programs operated by the Getty Trust will make important contributions to the visual arts and that their proximity may lead to new forms of collaboration as well as new knowledge in the field. Both the art collections that were shaped directly by Mr. Getty and the new programs of the Trust are tributes to his belief in the power of the visual arts in man's past and future.

In the months before his death, Mr. Getty was always eager to talk about the new building at Malibu and how it and the art collections were being received by the public. On one occasion he read aloud from a review of the new Museum by a British journalist, who concluded that Mr. Getty had built himself a fitting Taj Mahal. Mr. Getty paused, repeated the phrase "my Taj Mahal," stood, courteously thanked his guests for coming, and left the room. The journalist intended both admiration and criticism—admiration of the genuine achievement and criticism of the unusual aesthetic. But the comment was true in a broader sense as well. The J. Paul Getty Museum *is* Mr. Getty's monument, his gift to the future. In 1965 he had written:

> Banal as it may sound in this glib and brittle age, the beauty that
> one finds in fine arts is one of the pitifully few real and lasting
> products of all human endeavor. That beauty endures even though
> nations and civilizations crumble; the work of art can be passed on
> from generation to generation and century to century, providing a
> historical continuity of true value.

Although Mr. Getty never returned to the United States after May
1951, he maintained his domicile in California at all times and voted
regularly by absentee ballot. He spoke often of retiring to the ranch house
in Malibu and walking down to his Museum after breakfast. While he
never saw his Museum except in the photographs and reports of the
people who built it for him, he knew that posterity would preserve his
memory through what he had accomplished there, and in his will he
requested that he be buried on the Museum grounds. He rests there today
with two of his five sons, in a quiet spot that was a favorite of his,
overlooking the Pacific Ocean.

In 1984, a merger with Texaco dissolved the Getty Oil Company as it
had been conceived and nurtured by its founder. Mr. Getty's decision to
leave his name and support to an international cultural institution will be
a more lasting claim to immortality.

N.B. Mr. Getty's own observations as quoted here have been taken from the following
books written by or with him: *The History of the Oil Business of George F. and J. Paul Getty
from 1903-1939*, Los Angeles: n.p., 1941; *Europe in the Eighteenth Century*, Santa Monica,
1949; *Collector's Choice* (with Ethel Le Vane), London: W.H. Allen, 1955; Ralph Hewins,
J. Paul Getty: The Richest American, London: Sidgwick and Jackson, 1961; *My Life and
Fortunes*, New York: Duell, Sloan and Pearce, 1963; *The Joys of Collecting*, New York:
Hawthorn Books, 1965; and *As I See It*, Englewood Cliffs: Prentice-Hall, 1976.

ANTIQUITIES

Introduction

The beginning of the Museum's antiquities collection can be dated
to J. Paul Getty's first purchase of an object of classical art, a small
terracotta sculpture bought at a Sotheby's auction in London in 1939.
The thirty-eight years that passed between that time and Mr. Getty's
last direct acquisition, a marble head of a Roman youth, witnessed the
creation of a collection of ancient Greek and Roman art that had become
the third most important of its kind in the United States by the time
of Mr. Getty's death.

The collection's greatest strength is in sculpture; the heart of the antiquities collection remains, as when Mr. Getty was alive, the marble,
bronze, and terracotta figures, which represent an exceptionally broad
range of artistic achievement from the Greek and Roman periods. Many
of the Museum's most outstanding examples of ancient sculpture, including the dedicatory group with the portraits of Alexander the Great and a
companion (see p. 32) and the Tarentine terracotta group of Orpheus and
the sirens (see p. 33), were acquired under Mr. Getty's personal direction.

In the years since Mr. Getty's death, the collection has continued to
grow. Several major acquisitions of Greek sculpture have been made,
including the Victorious Athlete (see pp. 42-43) and a brilliantly worked
torso of a pugilist, possibly from Alexandria (see p. 35). Two very recent
and exceptionally important additions have been a Cycladic marble harpist of the Aegean Bronze Age and a statue of a standing youth of the
Archaic period.

Important acquisitions have been made recently in all other areas of
the collection. Particularly noteworthy are a number of Attic and Italiote
vases, several painted by master artists of the sixth, fifth, and fourth centuries B.C.; Etruscan jewelry; Greek and Roman gems and other engraved
material; and glass. The Museum has also acquired several fine examples
of Egyptian art of the Hellenistic and Roman periods and a number of
objects from the periphery of the Greek and Roman worlds. The central
focus of the collections, however, has been and will continue to be art of
the Classical period.

FEMALE FIGURE
Cypriote, ca. 2500 B.C.
Limestone
H: 39.5 cm (15½ in.)
83.AA.38

Among the earliest sculpted objects of aesthetic value to appear in the Aegean
and eastern Mediterranean areas, Cypriote female figurines range in height
from only an inch or so to slightly over a foot. The Museum's statuette is thus
among the largest known. With head raised, arms extended, and legs drawn up,
she appears to be seated or giving birth. An ancient break and repair can be seen
at her left shoulder. The stylized simplicity of the composition and the barely
modulated surfaces of her breasts and beaded ornaments combine to project an
image of direct and almost mystical power.

HARPIST
Cycladic, ca. 2500 B.C.
Greek Island marble
35.8 cm (14 1/16 in.)
85.AA.103

This statuette of a musician with his instrument was sculpted from a single
piece of stone with the simplest of tools sometime in the second half of the third
millenium B.C. We know too little of the culture of the Cycladic islands that
produced the harpist and the more familiar female idols to understand the purpose of these figures, but many of the surviving examples have been found in
graves. Unlike most of the other Cycladic musicians, the Getty harpist does not
play his instrument. Rather, he holds the curved frame of the harp with his left
hand and rests his right hand on the sound box. Some elements such as the hair
were originally added in paint, but in general, the modeling of anatomical
details has been artfully reduced to a minimum.

ELGIN KORE
Greek, ca. 470 B.C.
Asia Minor marble
H: 71 cm (28 in.)
70.AA.14

Among the finest marble statues in the Museum is the fragmentary Elgin Kore (ancient Greek for "girl"), once owned by the English lord who acquired the Parthenon marbles for the British Museum, London. The statue is representative of a type that was created in the mid-seventh century B.C. and continued to be made for almost 200 years. The kore wears a peplos with an overfold, a dress style current in Athens in the early Classical period, and grasps the folds of her skirt as she steps forward. Its apparently simple drapery gives an illusion of softness and movement.

GRAVE STELE OF A WARRIOR AND HIS WIFE
Greek, Athens, ca. 400–380 B.C.
Pentelic marble
102.5 x 43.3 x 15.3 cm (40⅝ x 17¹/₁₆ x 6½ in.)
83.AA.378

This stele stood as the marker above a family grave. The names of the deceased, Philoxenos and Philomene, are inscribed near the top. Philoxenos, clearly a soldier, probably fell in battle. The handshake symbolizes his farewell to his wife and their eternal union. Originally details of the figures—and perhaps of the architectural frame as well—would have been added in paint.

HEAD OF A GODDESS

(Athena?)
Greek, Magna Graecia, second half of
fifth century B.C.
Marble
H: 21 cm (8¼ in.)
82.AA.91

Carved from a small block of marble,
this head was part of a cult statue
whose trunk, arms, and legs were
probably made of wood. While the
hands and feet may also have been
of stone, the hair was of another
material. Such idols had only their
significant parts carved of durable
materials for reasons of economy and
were frequently dressed in woven
garments, which were replaced at
regular intervals.

CALENDAR OF GREEK RELIGIOUS FESTIVALS

Greek, Attica, early fourth
century B.C.
Pentelic marble
132 x 55 cm (52 x 21⅝ in.)
79.AA.113

This stele, carved only with regularly
spaced letters which were originally
painted, provides an important document of ancient Greek religious festivals. As an official calendar of the
community of Thorikos on the east
coast of Attica, it lists month by
month the festivals to be observed,
sometimes including the location for
the rites, and specifies the exact nature
of the sacrifices—the kinds of animals,
their sizes, and, often, their values—
and the responsibilities of the magis-
trates in charge.

TABLE SUPPORT IN THE FORM OF GRIFFINS ATTACKING A FALLEN DEER

Greek, Magna Graecia, end of fourth century B.C.
Marble
90 x 149 x 29 cm (35³/₈ x 59⁵/₈ x 11³/₈ in.)
85.AA.106

The motif of the weaker animal felled by stronger beasts was a popular one in Greek sculpture from the Archaic period onward, and one that became a metaphor for the opposition between life and death. In this group, two griffins, mythological creatures borrowed from the artistic vocabulary of the ancient Near East, are shown tearing the flesh of a fallen doe. Although the figures are sculpted in the round, the decorative symmetry of the composition (which serves to mitigate the brutality of the subject) and the concentration of the viewer's interest on a single side are appropriate to the group's function as an elaborate *trapezophoros*, or table support. The tops of the griffins' raised, sickle-shaped wings have been flattened to form a stable resting surface.

The abundant remains of brilliant colors—pink and blue on the griffins' wings, red for their combs and claws and the blood of the deer, gold for the deer's body, and green for the rough ground beneath the figures—provide an accurate impression of the group's original appearance. They also serve as a vivid reminder that most ancient sculpture was brightly painted.

HEADS OF ALEXANDER AND A COMPANION

Greek, last quarter of fourth century B.C.

Marble

H: (Alexander) 28 cm (11 in.); (companion) 26 cm (10¼ in.)

73.AA.27, .28

These two heads come from a sculptural group probably made as part of a large monument shortly after the death of Alexander the Great in 323 B.C. It is not clear whether the monument stood within a temple sanctuary as a dedication or over the grave of an honored person who may have been connected with Alexander's court. In either case, it was commemorative in nature. The two most significant figures, Alexander and his companion, were flanked by at least one female figure, a youthful male flautist, and a variety of animals and birds, fragments of which are preserved in the collection.

Although the sculptor's intention was to create an image of a deified hero rather than a realistic portrait of Alexander, the identity of the subject cannot be mistaken. Larger than the other heads in the group, Alexander's is recognizable by the characteristic leonine, billowing hair parted at the center and flowing down each side of his head; the eyes set deep under the bulging brow; the slightly parted lips; and the upward turn of the head to the viewer's right. The companion's portrait has been identified as that of Hephaistion on the basis of its similarity to a head on an inscribed stele in Thessalonika dedicated to him. Alexander's closest friend from childhood, Hephaistion was a competent military commander in his own right.

Abundant evidence of ancient re-cutting on the two heads as well as on the related pieces suggests that the entire ensemble may have been damaged in an earthquake and carefully restored.

SEATED MALE PLAYING A LYRE FLANKED BY TWO SIRENS

South Italian, near Tarentum, end of fourth century B.C.
Painted terracotta
H: (male) approx. 104 cm (41 in.); (sirens) approx. 140 cm (55 ⅛ in.)
76.AD.11

This unique trio has often been identified as Orpheus and the Sirens. According to classical mythology, the sirens were demonic singers who lured sailors to destruction with their beautiful songs. Orpheus, the most famous of all mortal musicians in Greek mythology, encountered the sirens on his voyage with Jason and the Argonauts to capture the Golden Fleece. In order to save the crew from certain self-destruction, Orpheus sang to the sirens as the ship sailed past them, and, mesmerized by his beautiful music, they forgot their own songs.

Although the fact that the seated male figure sings and plays a lyre has suggested his identification as Orpheus, his attire does not fit the usual fourth-century Tarentine representations of the Greek musician. On contemporary Apulian vases he is commonly shown in an elaborately embroidered Oriental costume, usually a long flowing robe with a short, capelike chlamys around the shoulders, and a soft Phrygian cap. Since the Sirens often appeared during the fourth century in non-mythological funerary contexts as mourners or as the muses of the underworld, this musician may be a simple mortal who wished to be remembered for his talents. Whatever his identity, the group surely decorated a tomb. Reconstructed from fragments, the figures are now being cleaned, and considerable amounts of color are being discovered beneath the dirt-incrusted surface.

LANSDOWNE HERAKLES
Roman, ca. A.D. 135
Pentelic marble
H: 193.5 cm (76 ³/₁₆ in.)
70.AA.109

One of J. Paul Getty's favorite pieces was the Lansdowne Herakles, found in
1790 or 1791 in the ruins of the villa of the emperor Hadrian (r. A.D. 117-138)
at Tivoli and until 1951 in the collection of the Marquess of Lansdowne. The
young Herakles is shown larger than life-size—as heroes and gods often were—
holding the club with which he slew the Nemean lion. Its skin, here held in the
hero's right hand, is an identifying attribute. Herakles was not only an examplar
of human achievement but also the subject of philosophical commentary, and
thus an appropriate model for a Roman emperor.

TORSO OF A PUGILIST

Roman, Alexandria, second
century A.D.
Parian marble
H: 58 cm (22¹³/₁₆ in.)
83.AA.11

Originally part of a standing sculpture
that may have shown the figure in
combat, this fragment lacks its arms
and lower body. The almost perfectly
preserved head, with its swollen ears,
and the upper torso portray the boxer
in maturity. The vigorous style recalls
the baroque current in Hellenistic art
that developed during the third century B.C. and flourished during the
second century in the western part of
Asia Minor and Egyptian Alexandria.

HEAD OF ATHENA

Hellenistic, Pergamon, ca. 165 B.C.
Pentelic (?) marble
H: 34.5 cm (13⁹/₁₆ in.)
82.AA.79

Although battered, this helmeted
female head is a fine example of sculpture from the very height of the
Hellenistic period. The massive forms
of the head appear somewhat static
and emotionally rigid, but the strength
of the depiction is undeniable. The
head was originally part of an over-
life-size, standing cult statue of
Athena. After being damaged at some
time in antiquity, the helmet's rim was
recut, and newly worked pieces were
carefully affixed with dowels.

KRATER

Roman, first century B.C.
Pentelic marble
H: (restored) 84.6 cm (33 ¼ in.)
82.AA.170

The Romans' fondness for decorative
furnishings is exemplified by this
bell-shaped krater whose carved relief
decoration depicts six dancing women,
three on each side. On the better-
preserved side, two figures dance
before a third playing double pipes.
Neo-Attic sculptors' interest was
directed toward artistic effect and the
design of individual figures within
harmonious compositions. They often
lacked originality and openly dupli-
cated existing designs, a fact under-
scored by the presence of a virtually
identical krater in the Metropolitan
Museum of Art, New York.

STATUE OF A ROMAN
LADY AS CYBELE

Roman, second quarter of first
century A.D.
Marble
H: 162 cm (63¾ in.)
57.AA.19

This seated figure represents Cybele,
mother of the gods. The lion at her
side recalls her mode of travel through
the countryside, either riding on a lion
or in a chariot drawn by lions. In her
left hand she holds fruit, which symbolizes her association with nature.
The mural crown, or diadem in the
form of a city wall, identifies her as
the founder and protectress of cities
and towns. The head is a portrait of an
unknown Roman matron of high rank
who must have been a priestess of
Cybele; combining specific features of
an individual with the statue type of a
deity was a common practice in
Roman portraiture.

STATUE OF A CENTAUR

Roman, ca. A.D. 90
(Centaur) rosso antico; (base) breccia
H: (centaur) 157 cm (61¹³/₁₆ in.); (base) 86.6 cm (34½ in.)
82.AA.78

This statue of a young centaur, preserved on its original base, was carved in rosso antico, or red marble, which even in antiquity was considered a precious material and expresses the extravagant taste of the Roman ruling class. A sumptuous example of decorative sculpture of the time, this centaur originally stood as a part of a group in a palace of the emperor Domitian (r. A.D. 81-96) near modern-day Castel Gandolfo in Italy. The mythical half-man/half-horse has a pigskin draped over his left arm; he grins broadly and holds a rustic syrinx, or pan pipe, in his other hand. As woodland creatures with a reputation for being lustful and overly fond of wine, centaurs often took part in the revels of Bacchus.

PORTRAIT BUST OF AN ANTONINE LADY
Roman, ca. A.D. 150
Italian marble
H: 67.5 cm (26⁹/₁₆ in.)
83.AA.44

The face of this elegant lady seems to convey a placid, yet intriguingly magnetic character. Although her face is unlined, she is no longer young; one detects the confident self-assurance of a Roman matron secure in her status. Her hair was finely carved in a careful arrangement inspired by the hairstyles worn by Faustina Major, wife of the emperor Antoninus Pius (r. A.D. 138-161). The intricate hair makes a rich contrast to the high polish—characteristic of Antonine sculpture—of her face. This bust's excellent preservation, deep psychological insight, and skilled carving make it one of the finest Roman portraits in the Museum.

PORTRAIT OF A BEARDED MAN
East Roman, second quarter of fifth century A.D.
Asia Minor marble
H: 28.5 cm (11¼ in.)
83.AA.45

Although it suffered losses in antiquity, this head from the Eastern Roman Empire is an impressive portrait of commanding presence. In a style common to other portraits of the era, the subject's hair was combed forward to form a thick mass turned under on the forehead and temples and backward to make a flatter roll at the nape. The sculpted volume is relieved only by lines that are chiseled lightly at the back and more deeply in the front. The features beneath the mass of hair appear delicate due to the translucence of the polished marble. Despite the damage on the lined forehead, at one time the brow bone obviously was prominent, as the cheekbones still are. The sunken quality of the cheeks below is accentuated by the mustache covering the upper lip and by the seemingly soft, textured beard that closely follows the jaw line. Especially compelling is the expression of the large, staring eyes, the dominant feature of the portrait.

FRAGMENTARY RELIEFS FROM A SHIELD STRAP

Greek, ca. 580 B.C.
Signed by Aristodamos of Argos
as maker
16.2 x 8 cm (6³/₈ x 3¹/₈ in.)
84.AC.11

This fragment is of monumental importance for the history of Greek art because it includes the earliest recognized signature of a metalworker in reverse across the background of the lowest panel. Since scholars have long debated the characteristics of Argive art, this relief is a valuable document both for the identification of an artistic personality and for the definition of an important regional style. In the upper of the two better preserved panels, a female figure is abducted by a male in armor with a drawn sword. The presence of the goddess Athena at the right edge of the scene may suggest that the two are Menelaus and Helen. In the lower panel, the inscribed names identify Herakles' bride Deianeira being carried off by the centaur Nessos.

FURNITURE SUPPORT REPRESENTING A WINGED FELINE

Ionian, second half of sixth
century B.C.
Bronze
H: 61 cm (24 in.)
79.AB.140

Ionian artists working on the western shores of Asia Minor during the Archaic period were influenced artistically by their Achaemenid neighbors in Persia. Although winged felines had long been popular with Greek artists, the angular lines of this creature, which was cast in one piece, suggest that the stylistic prototype was Persian. The struts projecting from behind the head and below the front paws indicate that this hollow bronze most likely functioned as the front leg of a wooden throne.

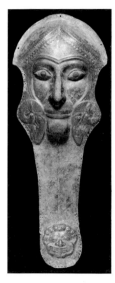

TRAPPINGS FOR TWO HORSES: HEAD PIECES
(*Prometopidia*) AND CHEST GUARDS

South Italian, end of sixth century B.C.

Bronze; ivory and amber inlay

(*Prometopidia* [original]) 45 x 17.2 cm (17^{11}/$_{16}$ x 6^{3}/$_{4}$ in.); (chest guards [restored])
approx. 107 x 25 cm (42^{1}/$_{8}$ x 9^{7}/$_{8}$ in.)

83.AC.7

Both the precious materials from which these trappings are made and their
beautiful decoration distinguish them as ceremonial armor, perhaps for one
of the champion chariot teams that brought fame to their owners in games in
Greece. Each head piece is made in the shape of the face of a warrior wearing a
helmet with ram's-head cheek pieces. Most details of the face and armor are
described with elaborate incision, and the eyes are inlaid with ivory for the
whites and amber for the irises. Each of the two chest guards is decorated with
an incised frontal quadriga. While the pole horses face one another, the trace
horses look outward toward the flying Nikai, or Victories, who carry wreaths
for the charioteer standing within the chariot box.

   Although the trappings probably date to the end of the sixth century B.C., the
style of the incised motifs seems somewhat earlier, especially in the treatment of
the hair of the Nikai and the charioteers, their drapery, and the frontal horses.
However, the materials used suggest an Italic origin, and creation in a provincial
workshop in Magna Graecia would help to explain the old-fashioned elements.
Two bronze helmets were found together with these trappings.

VICTORIOUS ATHLETE
Greek, fourth-third centuries B.C.
Bronze
H: 151.5 cm (59 5/8 in.)
77.AB.30

Few examples of monumental Greek sculpture have survived; among them, this bronze youth is an exceptional masterpiece. Representing a victorious athlete, the figure has one arm at his side while the other is raised to touch the victory wreath of olive leaves encircling his head. The wreath suggests that the subject was a victor in the Olympic games, and the sculpture, cast by the lost-wax process, may have been dedicated in the sanctuary at Olympia months or perhaps even years after the event it commemorated.

Although the artist is unknown, the style of the sculpture suggests the influence of Lysippos, a Greek bronze sculptor active through the second half of the fourth century B.C. The Getty bronze possesses a number of characteristics that have been associated with Lysippan style: an open stance, relatively unmuscled physique, small head in proportion to the body, and, in the face, a move away from the Classical ideal toward an approximation of nature. Despite the full and meticulous modeling of the statue, however, which indicates that it was intended to be seen from all angles, it contains only the barest trace of torsion. This evidently post-Lysippan compositional element suggests that the bronze may have been the creation of an artist living a generation or two after Lysippos' death.

STATUETTE OF ZEUS
Etruscan, Piombino, ca. 460 B.C.
Bronze
H: 17.5 cm (6 7/8 in.)
55.AB.12

Since Greek artists are known to have settled and worked at their various crafts in Etruria in northern Italy, it is not surprising that this small bronze Zeus should have an almost Greek flavor. Native Etruscan artists imitated the techniques and styles of the immigrants' craftsmanship so well that they became famous for their own work in bronze. The figure's left hand probably held a scepter or thunderbolt, both attributes of the king of the gods.

PORTRAIT OF MENANDER

Roman, late first century B.C.–
early first century A.D.
Bronze
H: 17 cm (6¹¹/₁₆ in.)
72.AB.108

This small bust is a copy after a Greek original created by the sons of the famous sculptor Praxiteles circa 290 B.C. The identity of the subject as Menander, whose image survives in about fifty ancient copies (including two in marble in the Getty collection), had been suggested but was unproven until this piece was published. The Greek inscription on the base resolved the question by naming Menander, the popular fourth-century-B.C. playwright of entertaining comedies. The outstanding craftsmanship and quality of the piece are especially obvious in the carving of the hair and modeling of the face.

HERM

Roman, first century A.D.
Bronze
H: 104.8 cm (41¹/₄ in.)
79.AB.138

Originally, herms were pillars surmounted by a bust of Hermes. These monuments, honoring him as a god of traffic and commerce, were set up in streets and marketplaces of Greek towns as well as on country roads to serve as milestones. A pair of stubby, arm-like supports, of which only one is extant on the Museum's herm, would have received floral offerings. Here the one preserved eye was carved in ivory and set between thin bronze sheets cut into eyelashes. The curly hair and beard are stiffly stylized although the folds of cloth atop the head appear soft and realistic. In the original composition, a bronze figure stood beside the herm, resting its arm on the folded cloth on the herm's head.

PORTRAIT OF LUCIUS CORNELIUS SULLA (?)

Roman, Asia Minor (?), first
century B.C.
Bronze
H: 29.5 cm (11¼ in.)
73.AB.8

A literary description and the striking
similarity between this head and certain early Roman coin portraits have
resulted in the tentative identification
of the subject as Lucius Cornelius
Sulla, the celebrated Roman general of
the late second century B.C. Said to
have come from Asia Minor, the head
was once attached to a full-figure
statue. It is the earliest Roman portrait
in the Museum's collection and is a
masterpiece of technical achievement
in casting.

PORTRAIT OF A LADY

Roman, late first century B.C./early
first century A.D.
Bronze
H: 16.5 cm (7½ in.)
84.AB.59

If one were not aware of its height,
one could easily assume that this
exceptional bust of an attractive
Roman girl or young lady is life-size.
Gazing slightly to her left, she is particularly striking because her eyes,
made of inlaid glass paste, have survived—an unusual occurrence for
ancient sculpture. Set on its round
base, the bust probably once stood in
the private shrine of a Roman house.

OINOCHOE

East Greek, Rhodes, ca. 625 B.C.
Terracotta
35.7 x diam. (body) 26.5 cm (14 x
10⁷/₁₆ in.)
81.AE.83

This trefoil oinochoe, or pitcher with
three-lobed mouth, is decorated in a
black-on-white style of vase painting
characteristic of the "Orientalizing"
period of the seventh century B.C.
This particular type of Orientalizing
painting is commonly called the Wild
Goat style after its most typical motif.
Subjects are exclusively animals, real
or imaginary, with floral and geometric motifs used as ornamental fillers in
backgrounds or framing borders.

HYDRIA

Caeretan, ca. 525 B.C.
Terracotta
44.6 x diam. (mouth) 22.9 x diam.
(body) 33.4 cm (17¹/₂ x 9 x 13¹/₈ in.)
83.AE.346

Although the labors of Herakles were
popular subjects in sixth-century vase
painting, the slaying of the hydra of
Lerna was not a very common representation. The hero had to kill the
many-headed sea monster by cutting
off each head and cauterizing the neck
so that new heads could not grow
back. Here the artist has included
Herakles' nephew Iolaos as an
assistant. Unlike Attic vase painters
of the same period, this possibly East
Greek master had little feeling for
the architectonic quality of the vase
shape. He also had little more interest
in the human subjects than in the
ornamental motifs.

PANATHENAIC PRIZE
AMPHORA
Attributed to the Kleophrades Painter
Greek, Athens, ca. 480 B.C.
Terracotta
65.5 x diam. (mouth) 17.5 x diam.
(body) 40.7 cm (25³/₄ x 6⁷/₈ x 16 in.)
77.AE.9

PANATHENAIC PRIZE
AMPHORA
Greek, Athens, ca. 340/339 B.C.
Terracotta
101 x diam. (mouth) 23.5 x diam.
(body) 39.2 cm (39³/₄ x 9¹/₄ x 15⁷/₁₆ in.)
79.AE.147

Every four years, the city of Athens held games as part of the religious Panathenaic festival. Victors were awarded amphorai filled with olive oil from the sacred groves of Athena. To distinguish them from other vase types, the prize amphorai were given the special shape seen here, which was to be canonical, with some minor variations, from the sixth through the second century B.C. The iconography, which was equally standardized, showed a striding Athena on one side and participants in one of the events, presumably the one for which the vase was awarded, on the other.

The confident outlines of the chariot group on the earlier amphora are filled with well-controlled energy, echoing the vase's taut profile. The later example, by an unknown artist from the middle of the fourth century, has replaced this energy with affected elegance. Although the horses are depicted with greater accuracy than those attributed to the Kleophrades Painter, they suggest a performance more than a heated race. Artistic vocabulary, restricted to formulae, has grown ornamental and devoid of content.

RED-FIGURE AMPHORA
Attributed to Euthymides as painter
Greek, Athens, ca. 520–510 B.C.
Terracotta
43.5 x diam. (neck [mouth restored]) 11 x
diam. (body) 25.7 cm (17⅛ x 4⁵⁄₁₆ x 10⅛ in.)
84.AE.63

The artist Euthymides was among the so-called Pioneers, the first group of artists to work in the new red-figure vase painting technique after its introduction
circa 530 B.C. In general a painter of large pots, Euthymides drew grand figures
with expressive outlines and organized his compositions with a fine sense of
balance. Athletes were favorite subjects, since the nude body in motion allowed
him to demonstrate his ability as a draughtsman.

On this vase, each side is dominated by a single figure: a discus thrower on
one side, a javelin thrower on the other. The name of the former, Phayllos, is
legible: this name is known from inscriptions on four other red-figure vases,
including two by Euthymides. Scholars have long speculated that this Phayllos
must have been the famous athlete from Croton in southern Italy, three times
winner of the Pythian games, twice as pentathlete and once as wrestler.

RED-FIGURE KYLIX TYPE C

Signed by Euphronios as potter;
attributed to Onesimos as painter
Greek, Athens, ca. 500 B.C.
Terracotta
Diam. (bowl [restored]) 46.6 x diam.
(foot) 20.5 cm (18³/₈ x 8 in.)
83.AE.362

Remarkable for both its potting
and painting, this fragmentary late
Archaic kylix represents Attic red-
figure vase painting at its best. The
grandeur of the subject, the Fall of
Troy, is appropriate to both the monu-
mental proportions of the cup and its complex scheme of decoration. Inside,
both the tondo and the large zone around it are filled with scenes from the sack
of Troy. Especially dramatic is the representation of Ajax's attack on the nude
prophetess Cassandra, who has taken sanctuary at the statue of the goddess
Athena. The artist has gone to great effort to provide an accurate narrative of
the Trojan cycle here, and he has carefully labeled his multitude of figures with
their names.

KYLIX TYPE B

Signed by Kleophrades, son of
Amasis, as potter; signed by Douris
as painter
Greek, Athens, ca. 490 B.C.
Terracotta
(Without rim) 12 x diam. (tondo)
24.1 x diam. (foot) 16.1 cm (4³/₄ x
9¹/₂ x 6⁵/₁₆ in.)
83.AE.217

Originally a very large cup, this fragmentary vessel is a wonderful document of the collaboration between a
master potter and painter, both of
whom signed it. The tondo presents a
courting scene. The younger beloved
holds his hand to his head in a gesture
of despair as the older lover looks on.
Although the paraphernalia hanging
on the wall at the left suggests that
the setting is the palaestra, or athletic
field, the pose of the seated youth
recalls representations of Achilles
sulking in his tent. The hole
through the center of the tondo
once held a metal rivet, apparently
an ancient repair.

KALPIS

Greek, ca. 480 B.C.
Attributed to the Kleophrades Painter
Terracotta
H: (with restored foot and mouth)
39 cm (15⅜ in.)
85.AE.316

The eminent vase scholar Sir John
Beazley has called the Kleophrades
Painter quite simply "the greatest
pot painter of the late archaic period."
A pupil of the Pioneer red-figure
artist Euthymides (see p. 48), the
Kleophrades Painter specialized in
grand compositions full of energy and humor. The unusual scene on the
shoulder of this kalpis, or water jug, is a superb example of his mature style.

The subject represented comes from the story of Jason and the Argonauts
on their voyage to capture the Golden Fleece. Blind Phineus, a mythological
prophet-king of Thrace, sits before a table piled high with meat and round
loaves of bread, trying desperately to defend himself from the three Harpies.
Because he had misused his gift of prophecy, Phineus was plagued by the
Harpies, evil winged demons who took or befouled all his food. The Argonauts
found him nearly starved to death when they arrived on their way to Colchis.
In return for his prediction regarding the future course of their voyage, the
Argonauts agreed to save Phineus from the creatures.

The kalpis is one of the most beautiful of all the Greek vase shapes, but its
continuously curving surface presented some obvious difficulties for decoration. In the hands of a master like the Kleophrades Painter, however, these
problems were transformed into strengths through the careful disposition of
figures and ornamental patterns.

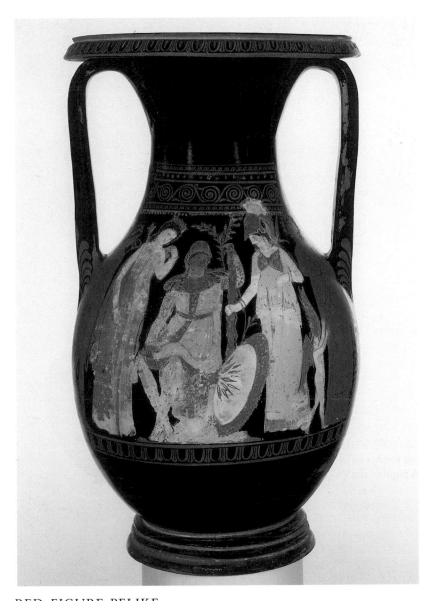

RED-FIGURE PELIKE
Attributed to the circle of the Marsyas Painter
Greek, Athens, ca. 350 B.C.
48.3 x diam. (mouth) 28.1 x diam. (body) 27.2 cm (19 x 11 x 10$^{11}/_{16}$ in.)
83.AE.10

Vases in the Kerch style, of which this is one, take their name from an area on the Black Sea where numerous examples have been found. The style is characterized by elaborate decoration, which often augments the simple red-on-black scheme of earlier Attic vases with combinations of polychromy, gilding, and relief work. The scene of the Judgment of Paris on the well-preserved surface of this pelike contains all of these elements. Perfectly suited to this elaborate ornament is the tall, elegant profile of this storage vessel.

FRAGMENT OF A BELL KRATER

Attributed to the Konnakis Group
South Italian, Gnathia, ca. 350 B.C.
Terracotta
10.7 x 11 cm (4³/₁₆ x 4⁵/₁₆ in.)
83.AE.431

Gnathian pottery, from Apulia in South Italy, is characterized by colored decoration applied over a black glaze. This fragment, to judge by the size of the figure, must have come from a rather large krater. The fragment preserves the head of a muse who would have been seated holding a kithara, a stringed instrument played with a pick. The painterly use of added color gives the figure a particularly vivacious appearance.

RED-FIGURE LOUTROPHOROS

Attributed to the Painter of Louvre MNB 1148, circle of the Darius Painter
South Italian, Apulia, ca. 340 B.C.
Terracotta
H: 98 cm (38⁹/₁₆ in.)
82.AE.16

According to ancient sources, vases of this shape were used for carrying water to nuptial baths and also as funerary offerings for those who died unwed. Thus their painted scenes are usually relevant to marriages and funerals. Here, in a naiskos, or small shrine, Niobe, whose children were slain by the gods after she boasted of her superiority to Leto, mother of Apollo and Artemis, stands slowly turning into stone. The vase's funerary significance is emphasized in the scene by two loutrophoroi within the shrine as well as by women making offerings outside.

RED-FIGURE CALYX KRATER
Signed by Asteas as painter
South Italian, Paestum, ca. 340 B.C.
Terracotta
H: 71 cm (28 in.)
81.AE.78

Since the number of vase painters who actually signed their work is very
small, it is relatively rare to see complete, intact vases carrying signatures. This
sizable krater from Paestum in South Italy is Asteas' major extant signed work.
It depicts one of the most popular myths in antiquity: the love of Zeus for
Europa, a mortal. Here the bull sent by the king of the gods carries her away
across the sea, alluded to by the marine creatures Skylla and Triton on either
side. Pothos, the personification of passion, flies overhead. Various gods,
including Aphrodite and Eros, deities of love, watch the scene from above like
an audience at a play, a composition not unexpected from Paestan artists, who
followed a tradition from Sicily based on theatrical associations of subject
matter and composition in vase painting.

PORTRAIT OF A WOMAN
Romano-Egyptian, ca. A.D. 100–125
Encaustic and gilt on wooden panel wrapped in linen
33.6 x 17.2 cm (13¼ x 6¾ in.)
81.AP.42

Painting was the most respected form of art in antiquity, but because of the organic nature of the materials from which they were made, the majority of ancient paintings have long since decayed. However, in the arid desert climate of Egypt, a remarkable group of painted mummy portraits has been found. Usually executed from life on a square wooden panel, the portrait was reshaped after the subject's death and incorporated into the linen wrappings of the mummy.

This fine example clearly illustrates its funerary use, for parts of the exterior wrappings are preserved. The near-perfect condition of the panel, which has been cleaned but in no way restored, is the result of burial conditions. At the same time, the liveliness, directness, and individuality of the representation support the hypothesis that this lady sat for her portrait sometime before her death. Her hairstyle and jewelry help to date the painting to the early second century A.D.

PAINTED SARCOPHAGUS
Romano-Egyptian, ca. A.D. 400
Tempera on wood
47 x 156 x 35 cm (18½ x 61⁷⁄₁₆ x 13¾ in.)
82.AP.75

A very rare type of Romano-Egyptian funerary portrait that combines two traditions—the mummy portrait and customary tomb decoration—survives on the front of this elaborately painted sarcophagus. The deceased reclines in comfort, attended by servants who provide him with food, cool air from a fan, and texts for reading. The smaller size of the attendants indicates their inferior social position. Similar scenes were often carved in relief on stone sarcophagi or painted on the walls of chamber tombs all around the Mediterranean. However, the expressive rendering of the young man's face is specifically related to the tradition of mummy portraits (see opposite). Fortunately, the sarcophagus was preserved with part of its contents. The variety of toys, bracelets, and toilet bottles and the elaborate leather slippers suggest that the deceased was a child.

FRAGMENT OF A WALL PAINTING SHOWING A NILOTIC LANDSCAPE

Roman, third quarter of first century A.D.
Tempera on plaster
45.7 x 38.3 cm (18 x 15¼ in.)
72.AG.86

This scene falls within the category of Nilotic flood paintings. A giant crocodile is about to attack a pygmy on a raft. Battles between pygmies and crocodiles had been popular subjects in ancient Greece and Italy for centuries, although whether they were intended as comic or genre scenes has never been fully resolved. The foreground drama is balanced by a monumental colonnaded façade on the far side of the river. Its phantom quality creates the impression that a dense atmosphere fills the entire scene.

PERSONAL SHRINE

Romano-Egyptian, mid-third century A.D.
Tempera on wood
(Isis) 40 x 19 cm (14⅛ x 14¾ in.); (portrait) 36 x 37.5 cm (15¾ x 7½ in.); (Serapis) 39 x 19 cm (15⅜ x 7½ in.)
74.AP.20–.22

The centerpiece of this personal shrine is the portrait of a man. The bust-length image, visible when the shrine was open, was probably done after death since the subject holds two funerary symbols, a wreath of rose petals and a leafy branch. The side panels are decorated with representations of two Romano-Egyptian deities often associated with life after death, Serapis and Isis. They would have been visible only when the shrine was closed.

REPOUSSE BAND WITH MYTHOLOGICAL SCENES
Greek, Sicily, 540-530 B.C.
Gilt silver
Approx. 8.5 x approx. 37 cm (3³/₈ x 14¹/₂ in.)
83.AM.343

Although small in scale, this band of gilt silver—possibly part of a ceremonial
belt—preserves a wealth of mythology in its decoration. The panels—of which
six remain—show complex scenes involving two or more figures alternating
with single large figures of running gorgons. In the first multi-figural composition, Zeus is locked in combat with the snake-legged giant Typhon, one of the
sons of the goddess Gaia, the Earth. The second scene comes from the cycle of
events that followed the Trojan War. Orestes is about to kill his mother,
Klytaimnestra, to avenge the murder of his father, Agamemnon; he has already
killed Klytaimnestra's suitor Aigistheus, whose body lies at his feet. The third
scene shows Perseus about to behead the gorgon Medusa. He averts his head to
avoid being turned to stone by the monster's face and looks back to his protectress Athena. In the final, very fragmentary scene, Theseus battles the Minotaur
while a woman, perhaps Ariadne, looks on.

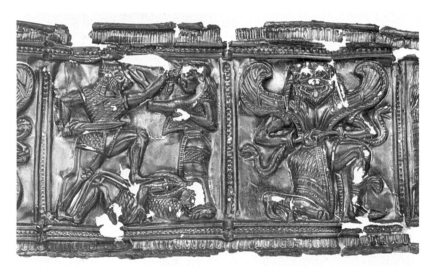

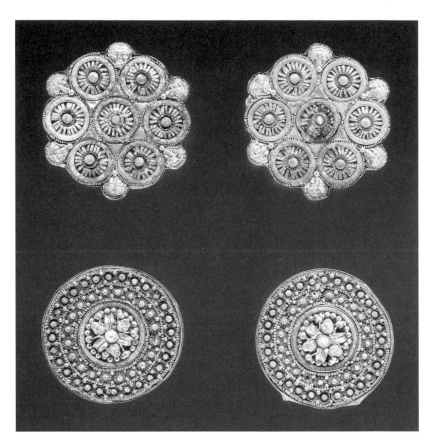

TWO PAIRS OF EARRINGS

Etruscan, ca. 525 B.C.

Gold

Diam. 4.7 cm (1⅜ in.); 4.2 cm (1¹¹/₁₆ in.)

83.AM.2a–b

Etruscan craftsmen were famous even in antiquity for the intricacy of their metalwork, and these two pairs of earrings show a remarkable range of gold-working techniques. From a distance, all look like rosettes. But upon closer examination, the large outlines break down into tiny components. How the Etruscan goldsmiths created patterns of such fineness in the seventh and sixth centuries B.C. without the aid of magnifying lenses has never been completely understood. Even the soldering technique for making the granulated surfaces that distinguish so much Etruscan jewelry has been a puzzle to scholars until recent years, and although the method is now understood, the effect is still quite difficult to reproduce.

BELT FROM A COLLECTION OF GOLD JEWELRY

Roman, end of fourth–early fifth century A.D.

Gold, glass paste, and precious and semiprecious stones

L: 76.5 cm (30 ¹/₈ in.)

83.AM.224–.228

Found together as a hoard, this group of objects presents a fascinating melange of materials and techniques. The individual pieces include two necklaces, three openwork bracelets, two chain bracelets, seven rings, and a belt made from Roman gold coins of various fourth-century emperors set into square gold links with green glass in the corners and an enormous central medallion inlaid with glass and semiprecious stones. The incorporation of pre-existing elements into many of the pieces—for example, the use of the coins for the belt links and of earlier intaglios in the rings—suggests a paucity of artistic creativity at the time of manufacture. It also presents some visual contradictions in the appearance of the objects; for instance, there is an interesting aesthetic conflict between the preciousness of the materials employed and the coarseness of their treatment. Yet the artlessness of these pieces clearly evokes the opulence and decadent splendor of the late Roman Empire.

SELECTION OF ENGRAVED GEMS

Bronze Age artists of the eastern Mediterranean from the third to the second millennium B.C. developed the tradition of glyptic art; they engraved small stones and other materials with a rich variety of designs. These amulets and seals were used as marks or "signatures" for personal use and were worn on clothing, around the neck or wrist, or set in finger rings. During the Archaic period, the Greeks revived the art of gem engraving, combining it with their own sense of artistic expression. New shapes, materials, and subjects appeared. Some outstanding examples are illustrated here.

The Museum has more than 450 engraved stones and rings in its antiquities collection. Most show mythological or figural scenes, but the collection also includes gems engraved with magic inscriptions. The overwhelming majority of the objects are from Greek, Etruscan, or Roman workshops, although there is a small and important group made by artists who worked in Achaemenid Asia Minor and in the coastal cities of Phoenicia.

(A) YOUTH ADJUSTING HIS SANDAL
Attributed to Epimenes as carver
Greek, ca. 500 B.C.
Cornelian
8 x 6 x 11 mm
81.AN.76.22

The scarab is engraved on the reverse with an image of a youth leaning on a stick as he bends over to fasten the strap of his sandal. The delicate treatment of the hair and facial features, the well-defined musculature, and the superior quality of the work are characteristics that secure the attribution to the great Archaic master gem engraver Epimenes.

(B) SEATED ZEUS
Greek, ca. 470 B.C.
Chalcedony
16.9 x 14 x 7.6 mm
84.AN.1.12

The scaraboid shape bears an intaglio representing the king of the gods seated, holding an eagle-tipped scepter, with a thunderbolt at his side. Although the artist is unknown, his work is of exceptionally high quality with meticulous attention given to detail.

(C) BUST OF A HELLENISTIC QUEEN
Greek, late third century B.C.
Garnet
19 x 13.8 x 6.3 mm
81.AN.76.59

The garnet is carved in shallow relief with the bust of a Hellenistic queen, probably Berenike II, wife of Ptolemy III (r. 246-221 B.C.). The portrait is very similar to those on coins issued during the reign of her husband. Although the practice of making cameos from layered agate was developed during the Hellenistic period, comparatively few examples of relief gems in other precious stones seem to have survived.

(D) HEAD OF THE DORYPHOROS
Roman, ca. first century B.C.
Dark green agate
Approx. (in setting) 22.4 x 17.3 mm
75.AM.61

The intaglio shows a profile head modeled after a famous late fifth-century-B.C. Greek sculpture, the Doryphoros, or Spearbearer, by Polykleitos. The artist's refined classicism reflects the taste of the late Republic and early Empire. The polished stone is of high quality, and the engraving is modeled with sensitivity and fidelity to the prototype.

PLATE SHOWING AN OLD FISHERMAN

Late Antique, fourth century A.D.
Gilt silver
Diam. 60 cm (23½ in.)
83.AM.347

PLATE SHOWING A PHILOSOPHICAL DEBATE BETWEEN PTOLEMY AND HERMES

Late Antique, fourth century A.D.
Silver
45 x 28.6 cm (17¾ x 11¼ in.)
83.AM.342

The two silver plates were found together in the sea and were probably made in the same late Roman workshop. They are splendid examples of the continuation of Hellenistic art into late antiquity, although they have considerably different styles and subject matter.

One plate shows an old fisherman removing a fish from his hook. In the background, two fish hang from a wall; the rest of his catch spills out of baskets around him. A line below his feet represents the edge of the sea, beneath which a variety of marine animals swim. The composition is enhanced by gilding and is

CAMEO GLASS SKYPHOS

Roman, end of first century B.C.–early first century A.D.
Glass
10.5 x 10.6 x 17.6 cm (4 1/8 x 4 3/16 x 6 7/8 in.)
84.AF.85

Roman glassmakers refined the technique of creating cameo glass by blowing glass of one color and encasing it in another, generally contrasting, color, which could then be carved by a lapidary in delicate relief. This process was time-consuming and very costly and resulted in luxury vessels for the wealthy. Few of these have survived intact.

The Museum's skyphos, or goblet, is one of only fourteen such Roman vessels known. It is remarkable for its large size and its similarities to the Portland Vase in the British Museum, London, one of the great masterpieces of ancient glass technique. Of the Getty skyphos' two principal scenes, the one visible here shows a satyr playing a lyre in front of a woman seated by a stele. His head is turned away, however, toward another young woman whose eyes are locked with his; leaning forward on a krater, she drinks from a bowl. Trees indicate an outdoor setting. On the other side of the skyphos, a satyr plays a lyre in front of a woman seated by a stele, but his head also is turned to look at another young woman. A facing head of an aged satyr is under each handle. Such scenes of satyrs, young women, erotes, or other figures drawn from Dionysiac mythology are common on luxury vessels of the late Hellenistic and early Roman periods.

---

surrounded by a rim of gold.

On the second plate an unidentified man is enthroned at the top. Below, a bearded man, designated by a Greek inscription as Ptolemaeus, is seated on the left; behind him stands a woman designated as Skepsis. Facing them is a man named as Hermes, but the inscription relating to the woman with him is lost. The subject seems to be allegorical, perhaps of the philosophical dispute between Science and Mythology. If this is the case, Ptolemy, the founder of the Alexandrian school of scientific thought, is seen here in debate with Hermes Trismegistos, the exponent of traditional human wisdom as embodied in myth.

MANUSCRIPTS

Introduction

In 1983 the trustees of the J. Paul Getty Museum inaugurated a
new area of collecting with the purchase of 144 manuscripts owned by
Dr. Peter and Irene Ludwig of Aachen, West Germany. The Ludwig
collection—begun in 1957—constitutes a nearly comprehensive history
of manuscript illumination from the eighth to the sixteenth century.
Approximately one year after the Ludwig acquisition, the Museum
began to expand the manuscripts collection in order to provide as complete and balanced a representation of European illumination as possible.
The collection represents the historical period between those covered by
the Museum's antiquities and European paintings collections.

Manuscript painting, which flourished from the end of the Roman
Empire into the Renaissance, was a major art form during the Middle
Ages. Illuminated manuscripts constitute the most complete record of
Medieval painting and generally have survived in extraordinary condition, with their colors as vibrant and fresh as when they were painted.
The illuminated manuscript was treated as a precious object, not only
richly painted but sometimes also decorated with jewels and the finest
metalwork. Such treasures were commissioned by rulers in both the secular and ecclesiastical domains. As the books of the Middle Ages, manuscripts provided the means for preserving and transmitting the basic
tenets of Western culture from its origins in antiquity and early Christian
thought. The variety of books in the Museum's collection includes liturgical and devotional texts, histories, romances, fables, and legal and scientific writing, and the schools of illumination represented include most
of those that flourished in continental Europe and Great Britain.

The manuscripts illustrated here are arranged chronologically, com-
mencing with the earliest of the Museum's masterpieces, the Ottonian
Sacramentary from Saint Benoît-sur-Loire, and culminating in examples
from the fifteenth and sixteenth centuries, including several Flemish
manuscripts (the Prayer Book of Cardinal Albrecht of Brandenburg and
the Spinola Hours among them), an area in which the Getty collection
enjoys particular riches. The illustrations in this handbook provide only a
suggestion of the complexity and luxuriousness of the manuscripts. For
example, the English Apocalypse contains eighty-two large miniatures,
and the Brandenburg Prayer Book forty-two full-page miniatures plus as
many narrative or decorative borders facing them. To show this variety
and to conserve both the bindings and colors in their decorations, the
Museum's manuscripts are exhibited on a rotating basis.

SACRAMENTARY

French, Saint Benoît-sur-Loire, first quarter of eleventh century
Vellum, ten leaves (ill.: fol. 9, decorative page)
23.2 x 17.8 cm (9⅛ x 7 in.)
Ms. Ludwig V 1; 83.MF.76

Containing the elements for celebration of High Mass, the sacramentary was
the primary liturgical book of the early Medieval Church. The regal illuminations in this fragment consist of a full-page Crucifixion and initial "D" (shown
here), three smaller initials, and two text pages. All are liberally embellished
with gold and silver gilt against unpainted or deep purple and black grounds.
Like the initials in the slightly later Ottonian Sacramentary from Mainz or
Fulda (see opposite), the complex interlace panels and foliate sprays in the initials and borders of this sacramentary hark back to ninth-century Carolingian
models based on Late Antique motifs. The entwined, climbing figures, on the
other hand, seem to anticipate the Romanesque taste for inserting human
figures and animals into manuscript ornamentation.

SACRAMENTARY

German, Mainz or Fulda, second
quarter of eleventh century
Vellum, 178 leaves (ill.: fol. 23, *Christ
in Majesty*, and cover)
26.5 x 19.1 cm (10⁷/₁₆ x 7¹/₂ in.)
Ms. Ludwig V2; 83.MF.77

The sacramentary containing this
Christ in Majesty also includes six
other full-page miniatures. These
illuminations typify the lavishness of
Ottonian illumination. The manuscript's luxurious binding in silver and
copper gilt, showing Christ in Majesty
in high relief, probably dates from the
twelfth century. Such an elaborate
binding reflects the sacred character of its contents and the special role the
sacramentary played in the performance of the liturgy. Indeed, rather than being
stored in a monastic library, this book was undoubtedly kept in a church treasury.

GOSPEL BOOK

German, Abbey of Helmarshausen, ca. 1120–1140
Vellum, 168 leaves (ill.: fols. 127v and 128, *Saint John Writing His Gospel* and decorated text page)
22.8 x 16.8 cm (9 x 6⅝ in.)
Ms. Ludwig II 3; 83.MB.67

The abbey of Helmarshausen was the center of the most advanced Romanesque illumination and metalwork in northern Germany. Each full-page miniature of a seated evangelist (Matthew, Mark, Luke, or John) in this volume faces a fully illuminated text page with the opening lines from the appropriate gospel. The illuminator's palette of purple, soft blues, greens, and salmon pinks is enriched with burnished gold and silver. Stylized geometric patterns express the body contours beneath the drapery of Saint John, who is shown here writing his gospel. This modeling, the decorative border elements, and the abstract patterning on the text pages closely resemble the style of Roger of Helmarshausen. Roger, probably Romanesque Europe's greatest metalworker, was a fellow monk of the illuminators at the abbey, which was patronized by Henry the Lion, Duke of Saxony (r. 1142–1180).

BREVIARY
Written by Sigenulfus
Italian, Abbey of Montecassino, ca. 1153
Vellum, 328 leaves (ill.: fols. 138v and 139, decorated initial "C" and text
page in gold)
19.1 x 13.2 cm (7½ x 5³/₁₆ in.)
Ms. Ludwig IX 1; 83.ML.97

The scribe of this breviary, the monk Sigenulfus, is identified in a prayer in
which he asks the Lord's blessing. Montecassino, where Sigenulfus copied the
text, was the founding cloister of the Benedictine order. The abbey is famous for
the illuminated initials in manuscripts produced there during the eleventh and
twelfth centuries; this breviary represents the tradition at its peak. Within its
pages are four full-page initials brimming with frenzied mixtures of interlaced
tendrils and actual or mythical animals (the initial "C" is illustrated here),
twenty-four half-page initials, and hundreds of smaller decorated letters. These
golden letters were inspired by the Ottonian illuminated initials in the Gospel
Book of Henry II now in the Vatican Library, Rome. That German emperor
(r. 973-1024) presented the latter to the Montecassino monastery soon after
his visit in June 1022.

GRATIAN

Decretals

French, Abbey of Saint-Colombe-les-Sens, ca. 1180

Vellum, 239 leaves (ill.: fol. 8v, decorated initial "H")

44 x 29 cm (17⁵/₁₆ x 11⁷/₁₆ in.)

Ms. Ludwig XIV 2; 83.MQ.163

Written circa 1150, Gratian's *Decretals* is considered the source of modern canon law, which governs the Church and its members. The Getty *Decretals* is one of the finest early examples and was illuminated within a few decades after Gratian wrote his text; it contains two full-page miniatures and numerous historiated initials, including this "H," in which male figures are intertwined with vines and monsters. A centerpiece of Romanesque illumination, the decorated initial encouraged the illuminator to give full rein to his imagination.

GOSPEL BOOK WITH LETTERS AND LIVES OF THE APOSTLES

Written by Theoktistos

Byzantine, Constantinople, Monastery of Saint John Prodromos, 1133

Vellum, 280 leaves (ill.: fol. 106v, *Saint John the Evangelist*)

22 x 18 cm (8¹¹/₁₆ x 7¹/₆ in.)

Ms. Ludwig II 4; 83.MB.68

A hallmark of classical antiquity—the naturalistic loose folds that express the curves and corporeality of the human form—is evidenced in the four twelfth-century miniatures from Constantinople in this gospel book. Set against the plain gold background often found in Byzantine painting and mosaics, the rich shadows and white highlights so sculpt the figure of Saint John the Evangelist shown here as to make the surrounding space palpable.

APOCALYPSE

English, Abbey of Saint Albans, ca. 1250

Vellum, forty-one leaves (ill.: fols. 5v and 6, *Saint John's Vision of the Book with the Seven Seals Adored by the Twenty-Four Elders* and *The Opening of the First Seal: The First Horseman*)

31.9 x 22.5 cm (12½ x 8⅞ in.)

Ms. Ludwig III 1; 83.MC.72

The abundant and inventive imagery of Saint John's vision of the apocalyptic end of the world, as recorded in the New Testament Book of Revelation, has inspired artists, including Dürer, Blake (see p. 136), and especially manuscript illuminators, since the early Medieval era. Illuminated Apocalypse manuscripts are among the most lavish productions of English Gothic artists and among the most popular; eighteen such examples survive.

The Museum's superb English Apocalypse, containing a commentary in red ink by the monk Berengaudus, has eighty-two half-page miniatures, one to each page. It has, therefore, the character of a picture book. Remarkable for their lively interpretation of John's vision, the miniatures are rendered in strong, graceful contours delicately modeled with colored washes. The elongated proportions, angular features, and decorative patterns of flat folds typify English Gothic illumination at its finest.

PSALTER

French, Paris, ca. 1250–1260
Vellum, 203 leaves (ill.: fol. 28v, initial
"B" with story of David)
19 x 13 cm (7½ x 5⅛ in.)
Ms. Ludwig VIII 4; 83.MK.95

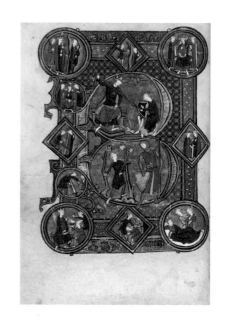

During the thirteenth century, Paris
was the reigning center of manuscript
illumination in Europe. This luxurious manuscript, with more than
two hundred miniatures, is decorated
in the court style of King Louis IX
(Saint Louis; r. 1226-1270). Characterized by miniatures in roundels and
lozenges and by an abundant use of
gold, the illuminated pages resemble
stained glass windows, an art form
which achieved its fullest expression
in Paris at the same time. This decorated initial "B" with *David and Saul*,
David and Goliath, and other scenes
embellishes the opening verses of
the Psalms.

BESTIARY and HUGO FOUILLOY, *The Aviary* and *Treatise on Shepherds and Sheep*

French, ca. 1270
Vellum, 102 leaves (ill.: Hugo
de Fouilloy, *Treatise on
Shepherds and Sheep*, fol. 46v,
The Good and Bad Flocks)
19.1 x 14.2 cm (7½ x 5⁹⁄₁₆ in.)
Ms. Ludwig XV 3; 83.MR.173

The bestiary, a Medieval collection of
animal lore, inspired numerous and
varied illustrated copies throughout
the Middle Ages and Renaissance.
This copy features a lavish program of
more than sixty miniatures, each
depicting a different beast, bird, or
animal story. Two essays by Hugo de
Fouilloy, prior of the monastery at
Saint Laurent-aux-Bois between 1152
and 1174, supplement the bestiary's
text. The work of the anonymous
illuminator from northwestern France
reflects a knowledge of the Parisian
illuminators of the day.

PSALTER
German, Würzburg, ca. 1240–1250
Vellum, 192 leaves (ill.: fol. 111v, *Pentecost*)
21.5 x 15.5 cm (8½ x 6⅛ in.)
Ms. Ludwig VIII 2; 83.MK.93

Richly illuminated psalters enjoyed widespread popularity as a form of deluxe
private devotional book in the thirteenth century. The palette, tall proportions,
and angular or "zigzag" contours of the apostles' garments in the *Pentecost*
scene—shown here unfolding under a symbolic church roof—characterize the
tradition of southwestern Germany, where Würzburg was a major center of
Gothic illumination.

   Probably the commission of a princely patron, the abundant decoration of
this psalter includes twelve illuminated calendar pages, each decorated with
the full-length figure of a prophet, followed by four full-page miniatures of
Old and New Testament subjects, two similar full-page miniatures, and ten
elaborate, large, historiated initials.

VIDAL DE CANELLAS

In excelsis Dei thesaurus (Vidal Mayor)
Spanish, Barcelona, ca. 1260-1280
Vellum, 277 leaves (ill.: fol. 72v,
illustration to "De Judiciis")
36.5 x 24 cm (14³/₈ x 9⁷/₁₆ in.)
Ms. Ludwig XIV 4; 83.MQ.165

This sumptuous manuscript is the
only known copy of a civil law text
written by the bishop of Huesca in
Spain. It was created in the royal scrip-
torium in Barcelona. One of only a
handful of works in the Aragonese
language, it was probably made for an
Aragonese ruler. The manuscript contains ten large initials framing miniatures as well as numerous smaller
scenes, mostly contained in letters. Its
style mirrors the Parisian court style
both in the settings and in the slender
figural and facial types enlivened with
primary colors (see p. 72).

GOSPEL BOOK

Byzantine, Nicaea or Nicomedia,
early and late thirteenth century
Vellum, 241 leaves (ill.: fol. 68,
Agony in the Garden)
20.5 x 15 cm (8¹/₆ x 5¹⁵/₁₆ in.)
Ms. Ludwig II 5; 83.MB.69

The abundant illuminations in this
gospel book probably were executed
in as many as three decorative cam-
paigns spanning the thirteenth century. The four evangelist portraits and
two other miniatures are all that
remain of the original decoration,
which is thought to have been
executed either in Nicaea or nearby
Nicomedia in the early 1200's. The
scenes from the life of Christ, including the compelling *Agony in the Garden* shown here, were inserted toward
the end of the century.

ANTIPHONAL
Italian, Florence, end of thirteenth century
Vellum, 243 leaves (ill.: fol. 2, *Christ in Majesty*)
58.2 x 40.5 cm (22¹⁵/₁₆ x 15¹⁵/₁₆ in.)
Ms. Ludwig VI 6; 83.MH.89

Choir books played a central role in the liturgy of the Church, providing the music for all the parts of the Mass or Divine Office that were sung by the choir. Richly illuminated examples were produced throughout Europe, many of the finest in Italy. This antiphonal, a choir book of the Divine Office, contains the chants sung by priests and monks at regular intervals—the canonical hours—of the day.

The manuscript contains a dozen large miniatures set into initials. These are composed in part of intricate, brightly hued vegetation and depict events from the life of Christ as well as portraits of apostles and saints. In their iconography, setting, and figural style, the paintings have a strong Byzantine flavor. Following the example of his contemporary Cimabue, who may have been his teacher, the anonymous illuminator directly imitated Byzantine or Byzantinizing models while making the figure of Christ more corporeal and human in scale and physiognomy than would have been the case in Byzantine art.

LIFE OF SAINT HEDWIG OF SILESIA (Hedwig Codex)
Silesian, Court Atelier of Duke Ludwig I of Liegnitz and Brieg, 1353
Vellum, 204 leaves (ill.: fol. 12v, *Saint Hedwig with Donors*)
33.8 x 24.5 cm (13⁵/₁₆ x 9⁵/₈ in.)
Ms. Ludwig XI 7; 83.MN. 126

The earliest illustrated *Life of Saint Hedwig*, whose subject was a thirteenth-
century duchess of Silesia, this manuscript contains one of the masterpieces of
Central European manuscript illumination: a full-page miniature of Saint
Hedwig herself. It depicts her barefoot before small-scale donor portraits of
her descendents, Duke Ludwig I of Liegnitz and Brieg and his wife, Agnes,
who commissioned the manuscript in 1353. Hedwig, who was canonized in
1267, founded a number of religious houses in Silesia, a duchy on the border
between modern-day Poland and East Germany.

The delicate features and serpentine curve of Hedwig's elongated torso capture the refinement of Parisian Gothic illumination of the fourteenth century
(see opposite), but the bright colors, heavy drapery, and full modeling of the
figure reflect an indigenous artistic vocabulary. Silesia's artists established a dis-
tinctive style with a wide influence on Central European art.

PETRUS COMESTOR

Bible historiale

Illuminated by the Master of
Jean de Mandeville
French, Paris, ca. 1375
Vellum, 308 leaves (ill.: vol. II, fol. 1,
Christ in Majesty)
35 x 26 cm (14 x 10⅜ in.)
Ms. 1; 84.MA.40

This luxurious Bible, with its delicate miniatures in grisaille against brilliantly colored, patterned backgrounds, represents the taste of the court of the French king Charles V (r. 1364–1380). The cool grays allowed artists to render figures as if they were carved from limestone. This *Christ in Majesty* framed by the four evangelists was placed at the front of the first volume.

CRUCIFIXION AND COMPANION MINIATURE

Illuminated by the Master of Saint
Veronica
German, Cologne, ca. 1400–1410
Vellum (ill.: *Crucifixion*)
23.6 x 12.5 cm (9⁵⁄₁₆ x 4¹⁵⁄₁₆ in.)
Ms. Ludwig Folia 2; 83.MS.49

The courtly elegance of the European International Style is captured in the rich costumes, brilliantly diapered backgrounds, and softly modeled forms of this *Crucifixion* and its companion miniature, *Saint Anthony*. Painted by the Master of Saint Veronica, one of the leading artists of the city of Cologne, these leaves may once have formed part of a devotional manuscript or have been mounted on panels to form an altar for private worship.

BOOK OF HOURS
Illuminated by the Master of
Guillebert de Mets
Flemish, Tournai (?),
ca. 1450–1460
Vellum, 286 leaves (ill.: fol. 18v,
Saint George and the Dragon)
19.4 x 14 cm (7³/₄ x 5¹/₂ in.)
Ms. 2; 84.ML.67

This deluxe manuscript, with gigantic, brightly colored foliage wending through its borders, exemplifies the inventive, often fantastic, and playful character of the decorative borders in Flemish manuscripts. The large scale of the acanthus dwarfs the elegant figures of Saint George and the princess whom he rescues from the dragon. The anonymous illuminator, called the Master of Guillebert de Mets, was a leading Flemish artist in the first half of the fifteenth century.

LLANGATTOCK HOURS
(Use of Rome)
Flemish, Bruges or Ghent,
ca. 1450–1460
Vellum, 169 leaves (ill.: fol. 58v,
The Annunciation)
26.4 x 18.4 cm (10³/₈ x 7¹/₄ in.)
Ms. Ludwig IX 7; 83.ML.103

Celebrated for a group of miniatures inspired by the Bruges painter Jan van Eyck, the Llangattock Hours is one of the finest examples of mid–fifteenth-century Flemish illumination. The jewel-like richness of color in this *Annunciation*, especially in the wings of the angel Gabriel, along with his delicate facial features and golden hair, are especially faithful to the Eyckian model. The identity of the illuminator, whose miniatures are rare, is unknown.

JEAN FROISSART

Chronicles (Volume Three)
Illuminated by the Master of the White Initials
Flemish, Bruges, ca. 1480–1483
Vellum, 366 leaves (ill.: fol. 87, *The Meeting of Popes Urban VI and Clement VII in Avignon*)
48 x 35 cm (18⁷/₈ x 13³/₄ in.)
Ms. Ludwig XIII 7; 83.MP.150

During the Renaissance, European rulers ordered deluxe illuminated histories, chronicles, and genealogies to celebrate their reigns and the accomplishments of their ancestors. This copy of Froissart's *Chronicles*, which was written in four volumes, was probably commissioned by King Edward IV of England (r. 1461–1483). Two companion volumes are in the British Library, London, while the whereabouts of the fourth is unknown.

A contemporary of Petrarch and Chaucer, Froissart was a French poet and historian. A welcome visitor at the ruling courts of Europe throughout his career, at age nineteen he had begun to write this account of the Hundred Years' War, describing the affairs of the rulers of France, England, Scotland, and the Burgundian territories. In addition to their intrinsic historical and artistic interest, the miniatures in the Getty volume provide a lively record of the stylish costumes and customs of the Burgundian court.

SPINOLA HOURS

Flemish, Ghent or Malines, ca. 1515
Vellum, 312 leaves (ill.: fol. 140v, *Massacre of the Innocents*)
23.2 x 16.6 cm (9⅛ x 6½ in.)
Ms. Ludwig IX 18; 83.ML.114

Unknown until a decade ago, the Spinola Hours is one of the most original
Flemish manuscripts of the sixteenth century. In many of the seventy-one full-
page illuminations, the decorative borders and miniatures are inventively combined into a single, unified space. In the *Massacre of the Innocents* shown here, the
landscape expands beyond the frame of the central compartment that normally
delimits the miniatures, extending into the border where subsidiary and con-
temporaneous events, such as the Rest on the Flight into Egypt, unfold.
Undoubtedly commissioned by a noble patron, this manuscript belonged to
the Spinola family of Genoa in the eighteenth century.

PRAYER BOOK OF CARDINAL ALBRECHT
OF BRANDENBURG

Illuminated by Simon Bening
Flemish, Bruges, ca. 1525-1530
Vellum, 337 leaves (ill.: fols. 147v and 148, *Christ Led before Pilate* and decorated
text page)
16.8 x 11.5 cm (6⅝ x 4½ in.)
Ms. Ludwig IX 19; 83.ML.115

The Prayer Book of Cardinal Albrecht of Brandenburg, a prominent art
patron of the Renaissance, is one of the finest illuminated prayer books by
Simon Bening, who was the greatest Flemish illuminator of the sixteenth
century. Bening's powers as a narrative artist are amply demonstrated in the
Passion cycle, twenty miniatures describing Christ's suffering, Crucifixion,
and Resurrection. In them, Bening's Christ is a sympathetic and vulnerable
figure whose physical torture is vividly conveyed.

GUALENGHI-D'ESTE HOURS

Illuminations attributed to Taddeo Crivelli, Guglielmo Giraldi,
and Giorgio d'Alemagna
Italian, Ferrara, ca. 1470
Vellum, 211 leaves (ill.: fols. 3v and 4, Taddeo Crivelli, *The Annunciation,* and
decorated text page)
10.8 x 7.9 cm (4¼ x 3⅛ in.)
Ms. Ludwig IX 13; 83.ML.109

This tiny, abundantly illuminated book of hours is one of the finest examples
of manuscript illumination from the school of Ferrara, whose ruling dukes,
the d'Estes, were ambitious bibliophiles and patrons of such artists as Andrea
Mantegna, Piero della Francesca, and Rogier van der Weyden. The decoration
is ascribed to three hands, those of Taddeo Crivelli, Guglielmo Giraldi, and
Giorgio d'Alemagna, the leading illuminators of the Ferrarese school. The
manuscript reflects the humanist values of the Italian Renaissance in the
classical details of the architecture, decorative putti, wreath, and scrolls.
It probably was executed in 1469 for Andrea Gualenghi, a diplomat at the
d'Este court and Orsina d'Este's third husband.

EPISTLES OF SAINT PAUL

French, 1520–1530
Vellum, 114 leaves (ill.: fols. 8v and 9, *Saint Paul* and decorated text page)
16.2 x 10.3 cm (6⅜ x 4¹/₁₆ in.)
Ms. Ludwig I 15; 83.MA.64

French illumination of the sixteenth century is noted for its combination of artistic influences from both Flanders and Italy. The floral border with naturalistic flowers, fruit, and insects is reminiscent of Flemish manuscripts, while the gold architectural frame, heroic figure type, and detailed landscape recall Flemish models that imitated Italian Renaissance art. This miniature accompanies the first chapter of Saint Paul's Epistle to the Romans.

Jan Van
Huysum fecit 1722

PAINTINGS

Introduction

During his lifetime J. Paul Getty purchased paintings from every major European school of art between the thirteenth and twentieth centuries. He did not, however, consider himself a collector of paintings. His writings, especially his diaries, repeatedly name the decorative arts as his first love. He also felt, not without some justification, that the best paintings were already in museums. Significant pieces of furniture, however, could still be acquired, and for much less money than a first-class painting.

Nevertheless Mr. Getty began his painting and decorative arts collections at about the same time: during the 1930's. By World War II he owned two major pictures, Gainsborough's *Portrait of James Christie* and Rembrandt's *Portrait of Marten Looten* (see p. 7), as well as a number of lesser paintings. Mr. Getty again began to collect paintings actively in the 1950's, although it was not until the middle of the following decade that he attempted to buy pictures that could be said to match the stature of individual pieces in his decorative arts holdings. Curiously, he never bought paintings to complement the French furniture he collected with such enthusiasm.

During the last decade of his life and until his death in 1976, Mr. Getty gave funds to the Museum that allowed it to acquire paintings from periods he had not previously found interesting. Some of these pictures are of considerable importance. When Mr. Getty left the bulk of his estate to the Museum, the opportunity presented itself to acquire major works on a wider scale. In the past seven years these pictures, which number nearly half of the paintings on exhibit, have significantly transformed the galleries.

During Mr. Getty's years as a collector, he succeeded in gathering a representative group of Italian Renaissance and Baroque paintings, plus a few Dutch figurative works of importance. In recent years these collections have been expanded. The French and Dutch schools have been much strengthened, and later French pictures by the Impressionists and their successors have been added. As a result, there is a greater overall balance of holdings from the earlier periods until the end of the nineteenth century. More significantly, the works that can now be displayed are often more representative and important examples than in the past.

It is expected that the Museum will continue to acquire and exhibit paintings of the highest quality during the coming years, to complete the collection's transformation from a fairly small personal holding into a moderately sized but exceptionally choice public repository.

SIMONE MARTINI
Italian, ca. 1284-1344
Saint Luke, after 1333
Tempera on panel
56.5 x 37 cm (22¼ x 14½ in.)
82.PB.72

Saint Luke, author of one of the Gospels, painted a portrait of the Virgin and
Christ. Painters adopted him as their patron saint and named their guilds and
academies after him. Here, Luke is depicted as the author of his Gospel, with his
emblematic beast, the winged ox, beside his inkpot. This panel, in its original
jeweled frame, flanked a central panel of the Virgin and Child. Its rich materials
and the curvilinear composition reflect Byzantine influence, but the extreme
precision of line and refined characterization are his own contribution to later
Sienese painting.

GENTILE DA FABRIANO
Italian, ca. 1370-1427
Coronation of the Virgin, 1420's
Tempera on panel
87.5 x 64 cm (34½ x 25½ in.)
77.PB.92

Probably painted for a church in
Fabriano, Italy, Gentile's *Coronation*
once formed part of a double-sided
standard carried on a pole during
religious processions. Stylistically it
occupies the borderline between the
essentially Gothic International Style
and the early Florentine Renaissance.
Traces of the former linger in the
richly patterned surfaces of the hang-
ings and robes, which, however,
clothe solidly constructed figures.
The folds create a sense of volume as
well as pattern, and the figures gesture
with convincing naturalism.

MASACCIO (Tommaso Guidi)
Italian, 1401-1428
Saint Andrew, 1426
Tempera on panel
52.3 x 33.2 cm (21 x 12 in.)
79.PB.61

This image of Saint Andrew holding
his traditional symbols, a cross and
book, comes from the only securely
documented altarpiece by Masaccio, a
polyptych painted in 1426 for the private chapel of Giuliano da San Giusto,
a wealthy notary, in the church of the
Carmine in Pisa. The panel belonged
on the right side of the upper tier, so
that Andrew once appeared to gaze
sadly toward the central panel depicting the Crucifixion.

The *Saint Andrew* exemplifies Masaccio's contribution to the founding
of an early Renaissance painting style.
The single figure is endowed with
volume and solidity; his simplified draperies fall in sculptural folds. Since the
panel stood high above the ground, the figure is slightly foreshortened for
viewing from below. Furthermore, Masaccio has abandoned the elegant
detachment of earlier styles in favor of a naturalistic treatment of emotion. It
was this powerful combination of three-dimensional form and bold expression
which so impressed his contemporaries.

BARTOLOMMEO VIVARINI

Italian, ca. 1432-1499

Polyptych with Madonna and Child, Saint James Major, and Various Saints, 1490

Tempera on panel

280 x 215 cm (110¼ x 84 in.)

71.PB.30

The saints in the flanking panels of this altarpiece have been identified thanks to their attributes. From left to right are: upper tier, Saint Mary Magdalen (ointment jar), Saint Ursula (banners and crown), Saint Apollonia (extracted tooth), and Saint Catherine (wheel); lower tier, Saint John the Baptist (rough clothes, lamb), Saint Bartholomew (knife), Saint John the Evangelist (book), and Saint Peter (keys). In the central panels, the Virgin supporting the blessing Christ stands above a full-length figure of Saint James Major, equipped with his pilgrim's staff and scallop shell. The prominence accorded James, the patron saint of pilgrims, indicates that the altarpiece may have been painted for a pilgrimage church in northern Italy.

VITTORE CARPACCIO
Italian, 1455/56–1525/26
Hunting on the Lagoon, ca. 1490
Oil on panel
75.4 x 63.8 cm (30 x 29 in.)
79.PB.72

On one side this unusual painting shows bowmen hunting birds on the Venetian lagoons; on the other, one finds a trompe l'oeil painting of a letter rack. The marks of hinges on the latter side have led to the suggestion that this panel once functioned as a window shutter inside a house. When the shutter was closed, inhabitants would see a view of the lagoon; when open, the shutter's back would blend with the walls of the room. If this explanation is correct, the painted lily visible in the foreground of the lagoon scene may once have stood in a painted vase on a parapet, which is now lost.

DOSSO DOSSI (Giovanni de' Luteri)
Italian, active 1512–1542
Mythological Scene, early 1520's
Oil on canvas
160 x 132 cm (63 x 52 in.)
83.PA.15

As court painter at Ferrara in northern Italy, Dosso was famous for his enchanting and mysterious landscapes inhabited by gods and legendary mortals. His dream-like, ornamental compositions embody the idealized Renaissance image of classical antiquity developed earlier by the Venetian painter Giorgione.

Just as his work on this mythological scene neared completion, Dosso changed his mind about its subject and painted a landscape over the draped female figure now visible at the center left. The three remaining figures—the sleeping nude, the protective central figure, and the god Pan on the right—may have represented the story of Pan and the nymph Echo. During the nineteenth century the fourth figure, whose significance remains enigmatic, was detected under the landscape and revealed by scraping away the upper paint layer.

VERONESE (Paolo Caliari)
Italian, 1528–1588
Portrait of a Man, ca. 1560
Oil on canvas
193 x 134.5 cm (76 x 53 in.)
71.PA.17

Based on the approximate date of the canvas, the age of the subject, and the physical resemblance to known portraits of Veronese, this painting has sometimes been identified as a self-portrait. However, full-length portraits of artists were uncommon in the sixteenth century, and the privilege of wearing a sword was rarely granted to painters. Whatever his identity, it has recently been suggested that the sitter may have had some connection with the church of San Marco in Venice, which appears at the lower left.

DOMENICHINO (Domenico Zampieri)
Italian, 1581–1641
Christ Carrying the Cross, ca. 1610
Oil on copper
53.7 x 68.3 cm (21⅛ x 26⅝ in.)
83.PC.373

Domenichino continually sought ideal form and grandeur, known as *disegno*, in his compositions; this painting is one of the earliest realizations of his goal. He often painted on copper plates, using small, controlled brush strokes to describe the massive volumes of the figures. As they lean over the fallen Christ, the tormentors embody the inexorable forces driving them to Calvary. Intent on their cruelty, they do not share in Christ's pleading silence.

GIOVANNI LANFRANCO
Italian, 1582–1647
Moses and the Messengers from Canaan, 1624
Oil on canvas
218 x 246.3 cm (85¾ x 97 in.)
69.PA.4

Painted in Rome about fourteen years after Domenichino's much smaller *Christ Carrying the Cross*, Lanfranco's composition displays the same concern for monumentality. His stark, powerful work shows the spies returning to Moses (shown at the left with his characteristic staff) laden with grapes and other proofs of the fruitfulness of Canaan (Numbers 13: 21–25). This picture formed part of a set of nine paintings (the Museum owns one other) representing Old and New Testament miracles involving food and hence prefiguring the Eucharist.

BERNARDO CAVALLINO
Italian, 1616–ca. 1656
The Shade of Samuel Invoked by Saul, 1650's
Oil on copper
61 x 86.5 cm (24 x 34 in.)
83.PC.365

Cavallino's late works on copper display the strange, brilliant coloring and delicate brush work suited to fantastical subjects. In this scene the shrouded ghost
of Samuel at the left warns the kneeling king that he will be killed if he goes to
war against David and the Philistine army the next morning (I Samuel 28: 7-25).
The witch of Endor, who has summoned the ghost, studies the king's face for
his reaction. This painting may have been one of four linked by the theme of
kings warned of assassination or death unless they changed their policies. The
unusual theme may have been inspired by the unstable political situation in
Naples, where Cavallino spent most of his brief career.

CANALETTO (Giovanni Antonio Canal)
Italian, 1697–1768
View of the Dogana, Venice, 1744
Oil on canvas
60.3 x 96 cm (23³/₄ x 37³/₄ in.)
83.PA.13

In Venice, the Grand and Giudecca canals meet at the point of land known as
the Dogana. Its eighteenth-century architecture included the church of Santa
Maria della Salute, whose dome rises at the background right, and the Dogana
da Mar, a customs warehouse, in the foreground. The ship flies an English flag,
perhaps in deference to one of Canaletto's many English patrons. Canaletto's
accurate renderings of famous landmarks made his work an essential purchase
for travelers who passed through Italy on the Grand Tour.

ALESSANDRO MAGNASCO
Italian, 1667/81–1749
Bacchanale, 1720's
Oil on canvas
118 x 148.5 cm (46½ x 58½ in.)
78.PA.1

Against the static forms of classical architecture, possibly the work of his collaborator Clemente Spera, Magnasco brushed in frenzied satyrs and bacchantes, followers of the god Bacchus. They are painted in the same monochromatic tones as the architecture and seem once to have been part of it, like the sculptures adorning pilasters and pedestals. Magnasco's agitated brush work and unnatural coloring heighten the scene's hallucinatory quality.

JOACHIM WTEWAEL
Dutch, 1566–1638
Mars and Venus Surprised by the Gods, ca. 1606–1610
Oil on copper
20.3 x 15.5 cm (8 x 6⅛ in.)
83.PC.274

In this small painting Wtewael has depicted a scene from Ovid's *Metamorphoses* (iv.171ff.) with appropriate raucous humor. As Vulcan (at the bottom right) draws his forged net from the bed, the lovers Mars and Venus (Vulcan's wife) reel back, Cupid and Apollo raise the canopy for a peek, and a gleeful Mercury (wearing a winged cap) looks up to Diana in the clouds at the right. Saturn (holding a sickle) and Jupiter crane their necks to behold the embarrassed adulterers. The rhythmically paired heroic nude figures show Wtewael at the height of his inventive powers as a Mannerist artist.

This tiny cabinet picture may have been painted for the private enjoyment of a connoisseur familiar with Ovid's text and capable of appreciating both the artist's skill and the significance of the painting's symbolic details.

HENDRICK TERBRUGGHEN
Dutch, 1588-1629
Bacchante with a Monkey, 1627
Oil on canvas
102.9 x 90.1 cm (40½ x 35½ in.)
84.PA.5

This devotee of Bacchus, with her fruit, nuts, and monkey (a symbol of appetite or gluttony), may represent the sense of taste. Caravaggio had set the fashion for half-length figures representing the senses in Rome at the turn of the century, and his works certainly influenced Terbrugghen's both in type and style. Coming from a Catholic city in largely Protestant Holland, Terbrugghen was one of the few Dutch artists to visit Italy in an era of religious controversy and so became instrumental in the spread of new Italian styles to the North. The lively, unidealized portrayal of the model and the sculptural modeling of her flesh in darks and lights are characteristic of the caravaggesque style Terbrugghen adopted while in Rome (1604-1614) and carried back to his native Utrecht.

REMBRANDT VAN RIJN
Dutch, 1606–1669
An Old Man in Military Costume,
ca. 1630
Oil on panel
66 x 50.8 cm (26 x 20 in.)
78.PB.246

From the beginning of his career, Rembrandt was occupied with historical, particularly religious, subjects. He soon took up a related genre, which he made his own: studies of individual figures in historical, theatrical, or Orientalizing costumes. Such works as *An Old Man in Military Costume* are not primarily portraits but rather studies of transient human expression, of costume, and of mood in which Rembrandt explored the diverse qualities of the human condition.

JAN LIEVENSZ
Dutch, 1607–1674
Prince Charles Louis of the Palatinate with His Tutor Wolrad von Plessen in Historical Dress, 1631
Oil on canvas
106 x 96.5 cm (41¾ x 38 in.)
71.PA.53

Jan Lievensz, a contemporary and collaborator of Rembrandt in Leiden, was strongly influenced by the latter's early work. This double portrait was painted in 1631, around the time that Rembrandt painted his *Old Man in Military Costume*. Lievensz, too, showed his sitters in quasi-historical costume and devoted his attention to their mood and character. His painting style also emulates Rembrandt's rich treatment of textures and dramatic chiaroscuro.

The subjects of this double portrait are thought to be Prince Charles Louis of the Palatinate and his tutor Wolrad von Plessen. The fancy dress of young Charles Louis—schoolboys did not normally wear laurel wreaths and gold-encrusted mantles—suggests a flattering comparison to an antique prince, possibly the young Alexander the Great, who was a student of the eminent philosopher Aristotle.

REMBRANDT VAN RIJN
Dutch, 1606–1669
Saint Bartholomew, 1661
Oil on canvas
86.5 x 75.5 cm (34 ⅛ x 29 ¾ in.)
71.PA.15

Rembrandt's subject has been identified as Saint Bartholomew by virtue of the knife, instrument of his martyrdom, gripped in his right hand, but the actual sitter may have been one of the artist's friends or neighbors in Amsterdam. Rembrandt painted several deeply moving studies of such men in the guise of saints and apostles in the early 1660's. Somberly colored and expressively painted, the *Saint Bartholomew* is an examination of age and introspection. The momentary distraction of the *Old Man in Military Costume* (see opposite) has given way to the saint's profound absorption; his thoughts are far removed from the present. During the thirty years between the *Old Man* and this painting, Rembrandt's style also shifted from concern for surface effects to a probing analysis of form and structure.

JACOB VAN RUISDAEL
Dutch, 1628/29–1682
Two Water Mills and an Open Sluice, 1653
Oil on canvas
66 x 84.5 cm (26 x 33¼ in.)
82.PA.18

Jacob van Ruisdael, who was born in Haarlem, was about twenty-five years old when he painted *Two Water Mills and an Open Sluice*. However, at this age he already displayed the full range of his artistic powers. The painting conveys a sense of the grandeur of nature, a unified conception abounding in detail. Nature's permanence—rocks, trees, land—and its changeability—clouds, wind, rushing water—are contrasted here. Blades of grass and slender leaves appear to rustle in the breeze along the bank. The dense forest in the background suggests generations of growth and regeneration with minimal human interference. The timber, plaster, and thatch of the mill house are well worn by the passage of time and the shifting temperament of the weather. Man himself, represented by the figure with the dog on the left, is dwarfed by his natural setting.

PHILIPS KONINCK
Dutch, 1619–1688
Panoramic Landscape, 1665
Oil on canvas
138 x 167 cm (54½ x 65½ in.)
85.PA.32

Koninck's expansive view, like Rembrandt's drawings and prints of landscapes (see p. 133), combines real and imagined elements to create the illusion of sweeping space as if seen from a great height. Unlike Ruisdael and Cuyp, Koninck used broad brush strokes freely applied to suggest atmosphere and the play of light across the countryside.

AELBERT CUYP
Dutch, 1620-1691
A View of the Maas at Dordrecht, ca. 1645-1646
Oil on panel
50 x 107.3 cm (19³/₄ x 42¹/₄ in.)
83.PB.272

The contemplative calm of *A View of the Maas at Dordrecht* is enhanced by the artist's subdued palette of browns, whites, and greens. Thin layers of color applied in sweeping horizontal brush strokes describe the limpid surface of the river, while the thickly painted white clouds evoke the dense atmosphere of Holland. Boats and towns—Dordrecht on the right and Zwijndrecht on the left—appear to float together between the luminous river and liquid sky. Cuyp's evocation of the passive power of nature contrasts with Ruisdael's treatment of it as an active force (see opposite), yet both artists show man as subject to nature's pace and mood.

JAN STEEN
Dutch, 1626-1679
The Drawing Lesson,
ca. 1665
Oil on panel
49.3 x 41 cm
(19³/₈ x 16¹/₄ in.)
83.PB.388

FRANS
VAN MIERIS
THE ELDER
Dutch, 1635-1681
Pictura, 1661
Oil on copper
12.5 x 8.5 cm
(5 x 3¹/₂ in.)
82.PC.136

These two compositions are both allegories of the painter's art. The Steen shows
the interior of a painter's studio, cluttered with symbolic objects, while the
painter, his pupil, and apprentice concentrate on correcting a drawing. Several
of the symbolic objects in *The Drawing Lesson* also appear as attributes of Pictura, a personification of the art of painting. Along with her palette, brushes,
and statue, this figure wears a mask hung on a chain around her neck. The mask
may be an emblem of deceit or illusion (the painter creates an illusion of reality),
or it may refer to the dramatic arts (like the dramatist, the painter must invent
and "stage" convincing scenes).

PIETER DE HOOCH
Dutch, 1629–ca. 1684
A Woman Preparing Bread and Butter for a Boy, 1660–1663
Oil on canvas
68.3 x 53 cm (26⅞ x 20⅞ in.)
84.PA.47

The orderly geometry of Pieter de Hooch's interiors seems to mirror the disciplined and orderly lives of their inhabitants. In this work a woman prepares a meal for a young boy, whose hands are folded over his hat in anticipatory prayer. The school building glimpsed through the open door is probably his next destination. The human figures and the semicircular mullions in the windows enliven a composition otherwise composed of rectangles. Rectangular grids parallel to the picture plane (as in the window panes) or laid obliquely (as in the floor tiles) define a succession of receding spaces further differentiated into luminous and shadowed areas. De Hooch's cool lighting and detached treatment of his subject are balanced by the warm reds, yellows, and browns of Delft brick, tile, and wood architecture.

JAN VAN
HUYSUM
Dutch, 1682-1749
Vase of Flowers, 1722
Oil on panel
80.5 x 61 cm
(31³/₄ x 24 in.)
82.PB.70

AMBROSIUS
BOSSCHAERT
THE ELDER
Dutch, 1573-1621
Flower Still Life, 1614
Oil on copper
28.6 x 38.1 cm
(11¹/₄ x 15 in.)
83.PC.386

The mania for cultivating flowers in Baroque Europe fostered the development and popularity of flower painters. One of the earliest of these specialists, Ambrosius Bosschaert the Elder, has grouped flowers from different seasons— roses, tulips, forget-me-nots, cyclamen, a violet, and a hyacinth—along with insects equally beautiful and short-lived. Jan van Huysum's bouquet of a century later includes several of the same flowers and insects as well as a bird's nest. Both painters celebrated the decorative qualities of their subjects but also intended to provoke serious reflection on the transience of life and beauty.

ATTRIBUTED TO ROGIER VAN DER WEYDEN
Flemish, 1399/1400–1464
The Dream of Pope Sergius, ca. 1437
Oil on panel
89 x 80 cm (35 x 31½ in.)
72.PB.20

This panel, which once formed part of an altarpiece illustrating episodes from the life of Saint Hubert, depicts Pope Sergius dreaming about an angel's revelation of the assassination of the bishop of Maestricht. The angel gives him the bishop's miter and crozier and tells the pope to appoint Hubert to the vacant post. In the far distance at the right, the pope receives a pilgrim, possibly Saint Hubert himself, on the steps of Saint Peter's in Rome.

MASTER OF THE PARLEMENT DE PARIS
Flemish or French, second half of fifteenth century
Crucifixion, mid–fifteenth century
Oil on panel
48 x 71.5 cm (18⅞ x 28¼ in.)
79.PB.177

This panel and its two wings depicting the arrest of Christ and the Resurrection narrate the events of Christ's Passion and rising from the dead. Christ appears three times on this panel. On the left, Saint Veronica wipes his face with her handkerchief as he carries the cross to Calvary; he is crucified in the center; and on the right, he releases souls from Purgatory. The soul-crunching demon of hell on the right spreads darkness to blot out the sun and moon.

JOACHIM BEUCKELAER
Flemish, ca. 1530–ca. 1573
Miraculous Draught of Fishes, 1563
Oil on panel
110.5 x 211 cm (43½ x 83 in.)
71.PB.59

JAN BRUEGHEL THE ELDER
Flemish, 1568–1625
Landscape with Saint John Preaching,
1598
Oil on copper
27 x 37 cm (10½ x 14½ in.)
84.PC.71

Beuckelaer's painting seems to consist of two unrelated pictures: a brilliantly
colored scene of fishermen returning with their catch in the foreground and
three episodes from the miraculous draught of fishes in the background (John
21:4-11). The "spiritual" landscape is differentiated from the "secular" one by its
restricted palette and mysterious illumination.

Working thirty years later, Brueghel broke down these pictorial distinctions.
Saint John the Baptist is surrounded by a contemporary crowd, his forest is
European, and the magnificent harbor in the background is probably the Bay of
Naples. Yet Brueghel too cast a special light on the figure of the biblical saint.
Both pictures display the tension between spiritual themes and worldly values
that is an important characteristic of Mannerist painting.

ANTHONY VAN DYCK
Flemish, 1599–1641
Portrait of Agostino Pallavicini, ca. 1625–1627
Oil on canvas
216 x 141 cm (85 ⅛ x 55 ¼ in.)
68.PA.2

During his second visit to Genoa in 1625–1627, Van Dyck is known to have painted Agostino Pallavicini dressed in the robes of an ambassador to the pope. The sketchy curtain behind the sitter here bears the Pallavicini coat of arms; his dramatic robes surely were intended for ceremonial duties. Van Dyck emulated his master Rubens' rich and dramatic painting style but brought to portraiture a unique aristocratic refinement that transformed the genre.

GEORGES DE LA TOUR
French, 1593-1652
Beggars' Brawl, ca. 1625-1630
Oil on canvas
94.4 x 142 cm (37¼ x 56 in.)
72.PA.28

Although the subject of this early La Tour composition—a scuffle between two beggar musicians—is clear, its meaning continues to elude us. Scholars have suggested that the two troupes are fighting for possession of a lucrative street corner; that the scene was taken from the theater, possibly from a comedy; that the musician in velvet is unmasking the false blindness of the hurdy-gurdy player by squirting lemon juice in his eye; and that the painting is really an illustration of a moralizing proverb such as "Wretched is he who can find no one more wretched than himself." La Tour has illuminated his frieze of beggars with a cold light from above. His strange palette, his attention to unusual textures such as the tanned and wrinkled skin of the aged beggar, and his extraordinarily detached treatment of his characters made La Tour one of the most original and enigmatic artists of the seventeenth century.

VALENTIN DE BOULOGNE
French, 1591-1632
Christ and the Adulteress, 1620's
Oil on canvas
168 x 220 cm (66 x 86½ in.)
83.PA.259

Although Valentin seems to have drawn his characters from seventeenth-century taverns and guard rooms, they participate here in a precise depiction of an episode from the New Testament (John 8:3-8):

> And the scribes and Pharisees brought unto him a woman...and...said...Master,
> this woman was taken in adultery, in the very act. Now Moses in the law com-
> manded us, that such should be stoned: but what sayest thou?...Jesus stooped
> down, and with his finger wrote on the ground, as though he heard them not. So
> when they continued asking him, he...said unto them, He that is without sin
> among you, let him first cast a stone at her....

Valentin has created high drama by contrasting the direct gazes of Christ and the adulteress with the averted, embarrassed countenances of the soldiers and Pharisees.

NICOLAS POUSSIN
French, 1594–1665
The Holy Family, ca. 1651
Oil on canvas
100 x 132 cm (39³/₄ x 53 in.)
81.PA.43 (Owned Jointly with the Norton Simon Museum, Pasadena)

The traditional Holy Family, which includes the Virgin and Child with Saint Joseph, has here been extended to include the youthful Saint John the Baptist with his mother, Saint Elizabeth. Framed by the passive figures of their parents, the holy children reach out in a lively embrace. Six putti bearing a basket of flowers, a ewer, a towel, and a basin of water may prefigure Saint John's later baptism of Christ in the Jordan River.

   Painted in Poussin's late classicizing style, *The Holy Family* reflects his study of Raphael and antique sculpture. Poussin's intellectual approach to painting, his insistence on order and harmony among all parts of the composition, and his concentration on the ideal and the abstract contrast sharply with the dramatic style of the caravaggist painter Valentin (see p. 107).

LAURENT DE LA HIRE
French, 1606–1656
Glaucus and Scylla, ca. 1644
Oil on canvas
146 x 118.1 cm (57½ x 46½ in.)
84.PA.13

This is one of six scenes showing the loves of the gods executed by La Hire as designs for tapestries, which were woven at the Comans workshops in Paris before 1662. Because the tapestries were intended for sale outside court circles, La Hire created a simple design including only three figures (weavers specializing in nudes received very high wages) and a simplified, atmospheric background, which was easily executed in tapestry. La Hire's choice of the only poetic moment in an otherwise violent tale may have been due to the decorative function of the final product. Glaucus, struck by the beauty of the hard-hearted Scylla, is seen pulling himself out of the water to tell her the story of his transformation into a sea god. His touching gesture, revealing Cupid's dart planted in his breast, is an innovation by the artist.

JEAN-FRANÇOIS DE TROY
French, 1679-1752
Preparations for the Ball, 1735
Oil on canvas
81.8 x 65 cm (32³/₈ x 25⁹/₁₆ in.)
84.PA.668

De Troy, a painter of historical, religious, and mythological subjects, is best remembered for his invention of the *tableau de mode* showing elegant company in fashionable interiors. Inspired by the *fêtes galantes* of Watteau and his circle and by Dutch seventeenth-century genre paintings, De Troy depicted a group of gallants preparing for a masked ball. Their lavish dress and the fine furniture add to the opulence of the setting. The mood of hushed expectancy is enhanced by the flickering candlelight which illuminates the room.

This canvas and its pendant, *Return from the Ball* (location unknown), were commissioned in 1735 for Germain-Louis de Chauvelin, Minister of Foreign Affairs and Keeper of the Seal under Louis XV (r. 1715-1774).

JEAN-BAPTISTE GREUZE
French, 1725–1805
The Laundress, 1761
Oil on canvas
40.6 x 31.7 cm (16 x 12⅞ in.)
83.PA.387

"This little laundress is charming, but she's a rascal I wouldn't trust an inch,"
wrote the critic Denis Diderot when he saw this painting exhibited at the Salon
of 1761. The instant rapport Greuze's painted characters achieve with their flesh-
and-blood audience was the source of his success with the exhibition-going
public of his time and remains one of his great strengths today. The theatrical
and moralizing qualities of his work are of primary importance: where will
this young servant's bold appraisal of the viewer lead? Yet the painting's technical qualities also deserve notice. Just as sensual as the laundress' glance and
exposed ankle are the creamy brush strokes delineating the folds of laundry,
warm ceramic and wood surfaces, gleaming copper pots, and the woman's
youthful skin.

JEAN-ETIENNE
LIOTARD
Swiss, 1702–1789
*Portrait of Maria Frederike van
Reede-Athlone*, 1755–1756
Pastel on vellum
53.5 x 43 cm (21 x 17 in.)
83.PC.273

Still Life: Tea Set, ca. 1783
Oil on canvas mounted on board
37.5 x 51.4 cm (14³/₄ x 20¹/₄ in.)
84.PA.57

Because he always wished to represent three-dimensional objects
in space as realistically as possible, Liotard painted children and
tea sets in a like manner. He set
his subjects against plain backgrounds and then recorded their
appearances as faithfully as possible. His definition of volume through subtle
gradations of color and his brilliant descriptions of surface textures (velvet,
skin, fur, and hair in the portrait; porcelain, silver, liquid, and lacquer in the still
life) create the startling realism that sets his work apart from that of his contemporaries. Despite his preoccupation with superficial appearances, Liotard's best
portraits are as spontaneous and revealing as photographs. Here he has captured
the alert intelligence of a seven-year-old girl. Liotard called the same technique
"deception painting" when applied to inanimate objects, since its main goal was
to convince the viewer that the objects were real, not illusionary. The disorderly
Tea Set, if propped up on a table, might persuade the uninitiated that the meal
was already over.

FRANCISCO JOSÉ DE GOYA Y LUCIENTES
Spanish, 1746–1828
Portrait of the Marquesa de Santiago, 1804
Oil on canvas
209 x 126.5 cm (82½ x 49¾ in.)
83.PA.12

An English visitor to Spain described the Marquesa de Santiago as "very profligate and loose in her manners and conversation, and scarcely admitted into female society.... She is immensely rich." Goya has not attempted to flatter his sitter in this portrait; its beauty depends on the manner in which it is painted. Broad brush strokes create the deep and splendid landscape; the dress is matte black on black. Thick impasto simulates the glitter of gold braid on the sleeve, and the diaphanous lace mantilla is described with broad, flat strokes of shimmering color. Goya's expressionistic painting style sets him apart from most other artists of the age, who sought ideal beauty in their subjects and high finish in their technique.

THOMAS GAINSBOROUGH
English, 1727–1788
Portrait of James Christie, 1778
Oil on canvas
126 x 102 cm (49⅝ x 40⅛ in.)
70.PA.16

James Christie, founder of the London auction house that still bears his name, is depicted as if attending one of his own sales. Much praised at the time of its exhibition at the Royal Academy, the portrait epitomizes Rococo elegance and grace. The style's characteristic arabesques are found in Christie's relaxed pose, in the tree and foliage of the Gainsborough landscape he leans against, in the gilt frame of the painting behind it, and in the artist's accomplished, free handling of paint throughout the composition.

JEAN-BAPTISTE-CAMILLE COROT
French, 1796–1875

Italian Landscape, 1839
Oil on canvas
63.5 x 101.4 cm (25 x 39⅞ in.)
84.PA.78

Landscape with Lake and Boatman, 1839
Oil on canvas
62.5 x 102.2 cm (24⅝ x 40½ in.)
84.PA.79

Italy provided the inspiration and motifs for many of Corot's early works, just
as it had for another great French landscape painter, Claude Lorrain. *Italian
Landscape*, with its combination of antique ruins and scenery taken from different sites, its silhouetted cows, and its dancing peasants, is in fact deliberately
Claudian. The golden light falling on water and greenery is further reminiscent
of Claude's morning scenes. Also like Claude, Corot paired this work with the
contrasting *Landscape with Lake and Boatman* for exhibition at the Salon of 1839.

CAMILLE PISSARRO
French, 1830–1903
Landscape near Louveciennes, 1870
Oil on canvas
89 x 116 cm (35 x 45³/₄ in.)
82.PA.73

Here, in one of his largest and most ambitious landscapes, Pissarro has conveyed the subtle tonal effects of gray light on an autumn day. At about this time, painting in the open air, Pissarro adopted the then-novel practice of breaking up surfaces with loosely placed brush strokes. This revolutionary technique, the cornerstone of the Impressionist vision, helped to reveal how light and movement affect the perception of objects and to capture specific effects of time of day and season. Louveciennes has sometimes been called "the cradle of Impressionism," since Monet, Renoir, Sisley, and Pissarro executed important paintings in the area in 1869–1871. Pissarro's motif in this work is a group of kitchen gardens behind a row of mid-nineteenth-century houses on the rue du Maréchal Joffre.

CLAUDE MONET
French, 1840-1926
Still Life with Flowers, 1869
Oil on canvas
100 x 80.7 cm (39³/₈ x 31³/₄ in.)
83.PA.215

Following the rejection of his paintings submitted to the Salon exhibition of
1869, Monet spent the summer and autumn of that year in Bougival, a pleasure
resort near Paris. Here he and Renoir painted their celebrated open-air views of
the La Grenouillère restaurant that are considered an essential moment in the
evolution of Impressionism. The *Still Life with Flowers*, painted at Bougival at
this time, is another motif Monet shared with Renoir. In this painting Monet's
vigorous impasto and sensitive chromatic modulations combine with a feeling
for compositional structure that characterizes his greatest painting of the 1860's.

EDGAR DEGAS
French, 1834-1917
Dancer and Woman with Umbrella Waiting on a Bench, ca. 1882
Pastel on paper
48.2 x 61 cm (19 x 24 in.)
83.GG.219 (Owned Jointly with the Norton Simon Museum, Pasadena)

Unlike his contemporaries the Impressionists, Degas arranged his subjects into compositions of great formal beauty laden with emotional power. He returned frequently to favorite poses or figures, finding fresh significance in each new combination, viewpoint, or variation. In this pastel Degas may have intended the juxtaposed figures on the bench to contrast the brilliant, artificial world of the theater with the drabness of everyday life. If the suggestion is correct that the scene shows a dancer and her mother from the provinces awaiting an audition at the Paris Opéra, then a contrast between the ephemeral glamour of the opera dancer and the dreary respectability of the provincial may also be implied. Each woman is absorbed in her own thoughts, yet they share a sense of tension and anticipation.

HENRI DE TOULOUSE-LAUTREC
French, 1864-1901
Model Resting, 1896
Tempera or casein with oil on
cardboard
65.5 x 49.2 cm (25⅝ x 19⅜ in.)
84.PC.39

Degas' influence on the younger
Lautrec is readily apparent in *Model
Resting*. The high viewpoint employed
here by Lautrec is found in earlier
works by Degas including *Dancer
and Woman with Umbrella Waiting on a
Bench* (see p. 117), as is the abstracted
air of the model, whose face is barely
visible. Simplified shapes of furniture
lead the eye into the back of the
picture space in each painting. Both
artists worked in unconventional media which showed off their talents as
draughtsmen and colorists, and they favored themes of horse racing and the life
of Parisian women of the middle and lower classes. All the same, Lautrec's
painting could never be confused with that of Degas. The curvilinear composition of *Model Resting* is not found in the latter's work; these curves plus the lus-
cious palette and prominent brush work give this picture its characteristically
decorative quality.

PAUL GAUGUIN
French, 1848-1903
Breton Boy with a Goose, 1889
Oil on canvas
92 x 73 cm (36¼ x 28¾ in.)
83.PA.14

Paul Gauguin began his career under
the influence of the Impressionist
painters but soon developed his own
style, which was characterized by simplified, flattened forms and bold areas
of color. In *Breton Boy with a Goose* he
has enhanced the tones of a Breton
autumn into brilliant greens, yellows,
gold, and scarlet. The bright areas of
color contrast with the boy's melan-
choly air; turning his back on the ripe
fields, leaning against a barren rock,
he faces the wind, perhaps with pre-
monitions of winter.

LAWRENCE
ALMA-TADEMA
English, 1836-1912
Spring, 1894
Oil on canvas
178.4 x 80 cm (70¹/₄ x 31¹/₂ in.)
72.PA.3

Exhibited at London's Royal Academy
in 1895, *Spring* is Alma-Tadema's
largest and most ambitious painting.
It depicts a procession of Roman
citizens celebrating the Cerialia, an
annual festival dedicated to Ceres,
goddess of agriculture and fertility.
The artist's idealized conception of
ancient Rome as a city of marble,
flowers, beautiful children, and sober
men is evoked in the verse from Swin-
burne inscribed on the original frame:

> In a land of clear colours and stories,
> In a region of shadowless hours,
> Where the earth has a garment of glories,
> And a murmur of musical flowers.

Alma-Tadema's ability to create a
fantastic world, replete with authen-
tic detail and anecdote, has led to
comparisons of his work with
seventeenth-century Dutch painting.
His "Dutch realism" (Alma-Tadema
was born and trained in Holland)
could not be more different from
the visual realism of Impressionist
painting or the naturalism of Degas
and Lautrec.

DRAWINGS

Introduction

The Museum's drawings collection was begun in July 1981, after Mr. Getty's death, with the purchase of Rembrandt's red chalk study of a nude woman as Cleopatra (see p. 133). However it was not until a year later that the Museum started to expand beyond this initial acquisition and that the Department of Drawings was formed. The collection now contains approximately a hundred drawings ranging from the second half of the fifteenth through the end of the nineteenth century. The major objective is to build a representative historical collection, with special emphasis on the most important and brilliant draughtsmen in the Western tradition.

The Museum decided to develop a drawings collection because drawing is perhaps the most universal of all art forms. The genre embraces a wide variety of media, including pen and ink, different chalks, charcoal, watercolor, and so on. Drawing is probably the only artistic area in which virtually everyone has had some personal experience. Moreover, every painter, sculptor, architect, and printmaker has used drawings in studying nature or the work of other artists, in developing ideas, and as a preparatory device in evolving projects. In addition, some drawings have been made intentionally as completed works of art.

The drawings illustrated in this handbook demonstrate great diversity. The two Dürers in the collection consist of a highly finished and self-contained watercolor and gouache study of a stag beetle (see p. 122) and, by contrast, a more loosely drawn pen study of the Good Thief for a painting or print of the Crucifixion (see p. 123). There are a number of compositional studies for paintings, such as the works illustrated by Veronese, Poussin, and David; studies of individual figures used in paintings, such as the Carracci and Watteau drawings; a preparatory study for a stained glass window by Baldung; and a number of drawings made for their own sake as completed works of art, such as those by Bernini, Rembrandt (the landscape), Blake, Ingres, Goya, Millet, and Cézanne. It is not always possible to know the reason why an artist made a drawing; this is true of the Rembrandt *Cleopatra*, the Savoldo, and the Rubens. However, irrespective of intention, drawings bring one closer to the variety of an artist's inner thoughts and instincts than any other art form.

Drawings are sensitive to light and therefore cannot be exhibited on a continuous basis. Those on exhibition at any given time represent selections from the collection united by period, origin, or other common elements.

ALBRECHT DÜRER
German, 1471–1528
Stag Beetle, 1505
Watercolor and gouache
14.2 x 11.4 cm (5⅝ x 4½ in.)
83.GC.214

This startling image is characteristic of the artist's interest in nature and coincides with the more definitively scientific renderings of plant and animal life by Dürer's Italian contemporary Leonardo da Vinci. At the same time, this drawing presents a living form illusionistically, with the stag beetle casting a shadow on the plain ground of the paper as if actually crawling across it. The beetle was drawn with exceptional care, especially in regard to the modulations of tone along the creature's back.

ALBRECHT DÜRER
German, 1471-1528
Study of the Good Thief, ca. 1505
Pen and ink
26.9 x 12.6 cm (10⁹/₁₆ x 4¹⁵/₁₆ in.)
83.GA.360

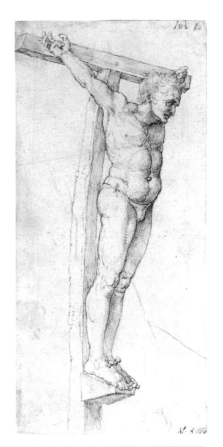

In this drawing Dürer conceived of the Good Thief with ingenuity and power. The figure is shown sharply foreshortened and at a rather stark angle, thus heightening the dramatic impact of the form. In addition, Dürer has shown the cross bending under the weight of the figure, whose hand, curled in agony, also reinforces the physical and emotive force of the drawing. The use of the pen here was completely assured and developed from the broad statement of the basic image to the clear definition and modeling of the forms.

HANS BALDUNG GRIEN
German, ca. 1480-1545
A Monk Preaching, ca. 1505
Pen and brown ink
30.8 x 22.3 cm (12¹/₈ x 8¹³/₁₆ in.)
83.GA.194

Baldung was one of the most distinguished of Dürer's followers. His characteristically rhythmic and sharply accented pen strokes were derived from his master. This drawing seems to have been made as a preparatory study for a stained glass window in a church, a type of commission Baldung is known to have undertaken. The preacher is depicted before his congregation. The presence of Christ above his left hand indicates that he is speaking on the subject of salvation or the Last Judgment.

RAPHAEL (Raffaello Sanzio)
Italian, 1483–1520
Christ in Glory, ca. 1520
Black and white chalk and wash on pale gray prepared paper
22.5 x 17.9 cm (8⅞ x 7¹/₁₆ in.)
82.GG.139

Raphael was one of the greatest, and probably the single most influential,
draughtsmen in the history of Western art. This study of Christ in Glory was
made from a live model, and one can still see the underdrawing of the undraped
legs that was rapidly sketched in first. The pose of the figure exemplifies
Raphael's classicism; the grand, idealized form is described with economy and
monumentality. At the same time, the artist used very subtle gradations of light
and shadow to give physical and spiritual resonance to the image.

ANDREA DEL SARTO
Italian, 1486–1530
Study for an Apostle, ca. 1522–1524
Red chalk
27.3 x 19.8 cm (10³/₄ x 7¹³/₁₆ in.)
84.GB.7

This sheet provides an opportunity to observe the characteristic manner in which Renaissance artists used figures drawn from models in their studios. Andrea drew his model nude, and when he came to use the figure in a painting—in this case, the *Assumption of the Virgin* now in the Palazzo Pitti, Florence—he added clothing and adjusted the pose. Andrea was one of the first artists to use red chalk regularly and did so with grace and subtlety.

PONTORMO (Jacopo Carucci)
Italian, 1494–1556
(Recto) *Saint Francis*; (verso) *Dead
Christ*, ca. 1517–1518
Black chalk with white heightening
40.7 x 28.4 cm (16 x 11³/₁₆ in.)
83.GG.379

This figure of Saint Francis was made
as a preparatory study for Pontormo's
altarpiece in the church of San Michele
Visdomini, Florence. The painting
was among the first Mannerist works
of art in Europe, and its elongated
forms and abstracting tendencies are
already present in this drawing.

Pontormo's ardent admiration of
Michelangelo is also evident in the
powerful and deeply expressive image
of the dead Christ. However, the very
personal character of the emotive quality and the violent angle at which the
head is thrown backwards are illustrative of the individualistic nature of
Pontormo's Mannerist style.

GIOVANNI GIROLAMO SAVOLDO
Italian, ca. 1480–1548
Study of the Head of a Bearded Man, ca. 1530–1535
Black and white chalk on blue or gray prepared paper
30.5 x 22.8 cm (12 x 9 in.)
83.GB.17

The directness with which this study of a live model was made belies its early sixteenth-century origin. It was probably drawn in Savoldo's studio from a model, perhaps for later use in a painting. The employment of black and white chalks on blue or gray prepared paper is characteristic of the colorist approach to drawing taken in sixteenth-century Venice.

LORENZO LOTTO
Italian, ca. 1480-1556
Saint Martin Dividing His Cloak with a Beggar, ca. 1530
Brush and gray-brown, white, and cream washes over black chalk
31.3 x 21.8 cm (12⅜ x 8⅝ in.)
83.GG.262

Due to the strong perspective angle indicating that one was intended to view
this scene from below, it has been suggested that the drawing was made as a
study for an organ shutter or a fresco above eye level. The dynamic movement
of the forms and the complex spatial organization of the setting anticipate
Baroque aesthetics of the next century, while the varied media employed here
are typical of the colorist tendencies in sixteenth-century Venetian art.

PAOLO VERONESE
Italian, ca. 1528–1588
Sheet of Studies for the Martyrdom of Saint George, 1566
Pen and brown ink and wash
28.9 x 21.9 cm (11⅜ x 8⅝ in.)
83.GA.258

This drawing is made up of a series of freely sketched studies for several sections of Veronese's altarpiece in the church of San Giorgio, Verona, showing the martyrdom of Saint George. This sheet reveals the creative energy of the artist as he explored varying solutions to different figural problems throughout the composition. He employed a combination of pen and wash with great sensitivity, and, although the sheet is made up of diverse parts, it comes together with a sense of the overall rhythmic flow of the artist's hand moving across the page.

ANNIBALE CARRACCI
Italian, 1560-1609
Study of Triton, ca. 1600
Black and white chalk on blue-gray paper
40.6 x 24.1 cm (16 x 9½ in.)
84.GB.48

Annibale made this drawing for his brother Agostino to use as the basis for a figure in a fresco by the latter on the ceiling of the Palazzo Farnese, Rome. The powerful sculptural form and the monumentality of the muscular image derive from ancient Roman sculpture and from Annibale's study of Renaissance art, while the use of black and white chalks on blue-gray paper reflects his interest in sixteenth-century Venetian art.

GIAN LORENZO BERNINI
Italian, 1598-1680
Portrait of a Young Man, ca. 1625-1630
Red and white chalk
33.2 x 21.8 cm (13 x 8⁹/₁₆ in.)
82.GB.137

This dynamic portrait of an unidentified young man is among the finest examples of Bernini's work in this genre. It was drawn with great liveliness, and the red chalk strokes show remarkable breadth and freedom. The use of white chalk, applied with equal vitality, adds luminosity and greater substance to the image. In this portrait Bernini has achieved an active interrelationship between viewer and subject; the young man looks out with boldness and animation.

L. Carache.   938

PETER PAUL RUBENS
Flemish, 1577–1640
Korean Man, ca. 1616
Black and red chalk
38.7 x 23.4 cm (15¼ x 9¼ in.)
83.GB.384

This is probably the portrait of a Korean who visited Antwerp. Rubens had close connections there with the Jesuit order, which was, in turn, active in the Far East. The drawing is one of the most meticulous of Rubens' portraits and is enriched by the use of color in the face. It is not directly related to any painted image by him and may have been made as an independent work of art.

REMBRANDT VAN RIJN

Dutch, 1606–1669

Nude Woman with a Snake (as Cleopatra), ca. 1637

Red and white chalk

24.9 x 13.7 cm (9³/₄ x 5³/₈ in.)

81.GB.27

This is one of the best preserved and most fluent of all of Rembrandt's red chalk drawings. He interpreted his famous subject as a living image, not at all idealized, and with great incisiveness in the characterization of her expression as she is about to kill herself by allowing the asp to bite her breast. The range of draughtsmanship in the form is quite remarkable, from the fine modeling of the right side of the figure to the virtuoso passages of freely sketched drapery at the left.

REMBRANDT VAN RIJN

Dutch, 1606–1669

Landscape (with the House with the Little Tower), ca. 1651–1652

Pen and ink and wash

9.7 x 21.7 cm (3¹³/₁₆ x 8⁹/₁₆ in.)

83.GA.363

This is among the most sensitive of Rembrandt's landscape drawings and one of his most experimental. He created the suggestion of space and atmosphere in the foreground through the use of a very few lines. Then, with a complex mixture of thin lines, dotting, and a varied wash, he elaborated a rich and diverse background. The quality of air and light in this sheet is remarkable. It is a prime example of a great artist evoking a vast and varied ambience with economy of means.

NICOLAS POUSSIN
French, 1594–1665
Apollo and the Muses on Parnassus, ca. 1626–1632
Pen and brown ink and brown wash
17.8 x 24.6 cm (7 x 9 ¹¹/₁₆ in.)
83.GG.345

Poussin was an admirer of Raphael and of the entire classical tradition. This
drawing is based on the famous fresco by Raphael in the Stanza della Segnatura
in the Vatican. The drawing is unusually animated for Poussin but shows his
characteristic tendency to abstract forms and to employ wash quite broadly. He
used this study in formulating a painting now in the Museo del Prado, Madrid.

JEAN-ANTOINE WATTEAU
French, 1684–1721
Seated Woman with a Fan, ca. 1717
Red, black, and white chalk on light brown paper
18.5 x 21.5 cm (7 5/16 x 8 7/16 in.)
82.GB.164

Watteau often made studies of this kind to use as the basis for figures in one or more paintings, most clearly in a painting entitled *The Timid Lover*, now in the Palacio Real, Madrid. The woman in the Museum's drawing appears several times in his painted work. The drawing was made in three colors of chalk, the medium for which Watteau is most admired and that best expresses his rich colorism in drawing. The study is exceptionally well preserved and shows great subtlety of surface texture.

JACQUES-LOUIS DAVID
French, 1748–1825
The Lictors Carrying the Bodies of the Sons of Brutus, 1787
Pen and ink and wash
32.5 x 42 cm (13 13/16 x 16 1/2 in.)
84.GA.8

In this drawing David has depicted a scene from ancient Roman history that is emblematic of great moral and patriotic virtue. Brutus, who has condemned his sons to death for treason, sits stoically in the foreground contemplating the tragedy while their bodies are carried away at the left and his wife and daughters mourn at the right. The drawing is highly finished, and its composition was employed, with changes, in David's painting of the same theme now in the Musée du Louvre, Paris. This is among the most monumental and complete of David's drawings.

WILLIAM BLAKE
English, 1757–1827
Satan Exulting over Eve, 1795
Pencil, pen, and watercolor over color print
39.8 x 53.2 cm (15^{11}/$_{16}$ x 20^{15}/$_{16}$ in.)
84.GC.49

This is a powerful example of the art of Blake, inspired both by the Bible and his own Miltonian approach to it. Although a fine technician, Blake preferred broadly executed compositions of this kind, intentionally avoiding the naturalism of form and space refined by Western artists before him.

FRANCISCO JOSÉ DE
GOYA Y LUCIENTES
Spanish, 1746–1828
Contemptuous of the Insults, ca.
1808–1812
Brush and india ink wash
26.4 x 18.5 cm (10^{3}/$_{8}$ x 7^{1}/$_{4}$ in.)
82.DG.96

This sheet was once part of an album of drawings that Goya seems to have made for his private use. Drawn with great tonal subtlety and fluidity, it shows a gentleman expressing disdain for the insults of gnomes, possibly a symbol of Goya's contempt for the soldiers who caused great devastation in Spain during the Napoleonic wars.

JEAN-AUGUST-DOMINIQUE INGRES
French, 1780–1867
Portrait of Lord Grantham, 1816
Pencil
39.8 x 26.2 cm (15³/₄ x 10³/₈ in.)
82.GD.106

Lord Grantham was an Englishman who visited Rome and commissioned this
drawn portrait from Ingres. It shows the subject standing in front of a distant
view of Saint Peter's and exemplifies Ingres' refined manner and purity of line.
At the same time, it shows great linear variety, ranging from thin, very fine
strokes to bold and heavy areas. The general restraint in graphic manner is fully
in accord with the portrayal of the subject.

JEAN-FRANÇOIS MILLET
French, 1814–1875
Shepherdess and Her Flock, 1865–1866
Charcoal and pastel
36.4 x 47.2 cm (14 5/16 x 18 5/8 in.)
83.GF.220

Millet is best known for his depiction of rural peasant life. This large drawing in charcoal and pastel monumentalizes the young shepherdess who stands with classical restraint in an idealized rendering of everyday pastoral existence. One of the most striking details in the drawing is the small dog at the right, whose sharp profile establishes a clear reference point in space and whose absolute blackness acts as an accent in the context of the generally dark tonality of the scene.

PAUL CEZANNE
French, 1839-1906
Still Life, ca. 1900
Watercolor over pencil
47.8 x 63 cm (18⅛ x 24⅞ in.)
83.GC.221

This is one of the largest and most ambitious of all of Cézanne's watercolors. It is very highly worked up, and in this respect, as in its scale, it shares the character of his paintings. At the same time, the richness of technique, with levels of translucent watercolor creating both carefully structured forms and veils of colored light, brings out the possibilities of this medium to the fullest. It is noteworthy that the almost kaleidoscopic effects of color enhance the monumental purity of the blank white areas of the paper. In every respect this is one of the artist's most accomplished works in drawing.

DECORATIVE ARTS

Introduction

The Museum's collection of decorative arts—of which less than a quarter is illustrated here—consists mainly of objects made in Paris from the mid-seventeenth to the end of the nineteenth century. It contains furniture, silver, ceramics, tapestries, carpets, and objects made of gilt bronze. The latter include wall lights, chandeliers, firedogs, and ink-stands. All of these objects are displayed in the Museum in chronological order, together with suitable paintings and sculpture, in twelve galleries, three of which are fitted with eighteenth-century paneling to form period rooms. Some pieces of furniture are also to be found in the paint-ing galleries.

J. Paul Getty began to acquire furniture in the late 1930's and continued to acquire slowly until the 1960's. Then, having opened his original small museum in Malibu, he stopped collecting for a time. At this point the entire collection of decorative arts was housed in two galleries. The thirty-odd good pieces represented the entire spectrum of eighteenth-century craftsmanship in Paris.

With the prospect of filling the much larger museum that was to open in 1974, Mr. Getty began to acquire again in the early 1970's and con-tinued to do so until his death in 1976. In this period strong roots were put down, and some new curatorial policies were established. Gradually a conception began to be realized, that of forming a representative collec-tion of French decorative arts from the early years of the reign of Louis XIV (1643-1715) through the early decades of the nineteenth century, known as the Empire period.

With the formation of the J. Paul Getty Trust, the confines of the col-lection were expanded to include objects made in Germany as well as those from Italy and, more recently, Northern Europe. The time span covered by the collection has also been extended. It is to be expected that this expansion of the decorative arts collection will take place slowly. In keeping with the standards already set, only the finest pieces will be acquired, to be gleaned from a slender international market that is often restricted by laws pertaining to legal exportation. The expansion of the collection will obviously outstrip the space presently provided to house it. As new objects are acquired, therefore, other objects will be removed into storage. Thus the galleries will be ever-changing, and visitors returning to the Museum will be rewarded by the sight of new objects.

READING AND WRITING TABLE
French, Paris, ca. 1670–1675
Oak veneered with ivory, horn, and ebony; gilt bronze moldings
63.5 x 48.5 x 35.5 cm (2 ft. 1 in. x 1 ft. 7^{1}/$_{8}$ in. x 1 ft. 2 in.)
83.DA.21

This small table, described in the posthumous inventory of Louis XIV, is one
of the few surviving pieces of furniture to have belonged to that great monarch.
Among the rarest and earliest pieces in the collection, it is decorated with
horn painted blue underneath, perhaps to resemble lapis lazuli. The table is
fitted with an adjustable writing surface and a drawer constructed to contain
writing equipment.

ONE OF TWO COFFERS ON STANDS
Attributed to André-Charles Boulle
French, Paris, ca. 1680–1685
Oak veneered with brass, pewter, tortoiseshell, and ebony; gilt bronze mounts
156.6 x 89.9 x 55.9 cm (5 ft. 1⅛ in. x 2 ft. 11⅜ in. x 1 ft. 10 in.)
82.DA.109.1–.2

This coffer and its pendant were almost certainly made by Boulle at a time
when he was making numerous pieces of furniture for the Grand Dauphin, son
of Louis XIV. A coffer of similar form delivered by Boulle is listed in the Grand
Dauphin's inventory of 1689. Such coffers were intended to hold jewelry and
other precious objects. The large gilt bronze straps at the front of this one can be
let down to reveal small drawers.

TABLE

French, Paris, ca. 1680
Oak veneered with brass, pewter, tortoiseshell, ebony, and olive wood; gilded wood and gilt bronze mounts
76.7 x 42 x 36.1 cm (2 ft. 6½ in. x 1 ft. 4½ in. x 1 ft. 2¼ in.)
82.DA.34

The top of this small table folds open to reveal a scene of two women taking tea beneath a canopy. It is therefore likely that the table was intended to support a tea tray. The table is decorated with two large dolphins and four fleurs-de-lis, all in tortoiseshell. These emblems were used by the Grand Dauphin, son of Louis XIV, for whom this table and its pair, now in the British Royal Collection, probably were made. The scene on the top was taken from an engraving by the Huguenot ornamentalist and engraver Daniel Marot.

CABINET ON STAND

French, Gobelins (?), ca. 1675-1680
Oak veneered with pewter, brass, tortoiseshell, horn, ebony, ivory, and wood marquetry; bronze mounts; painted, gilded figures
230 x 151.2 x 66.7 cm (7 ft. 6½ in. x 4 ft. 11½ in. x 2 ft. 2¼ in.)
77.DA.1

This cabinet was probably made at the Gobelins manufactory for Louis XIV, whose likeness appears in a bronze medallion above the central door, or for a royal gift. The medallion is flanked by military trophies, while the marquetry on the door below shows the cockerel of France triumphant over the eagle of the Holy Roman Empire and the lion of Spain and the Spanish Netherlands. The cabinet is supported by two large figures, the one on the right being Hercules. Clearly made to glorify Louis XIV's victories, this piece is one of a pair; the other is privately owned.

TABLE

French, Gobelins (?), ca. 1680

Oak veneered with brass, pewter, tortoiseshell, ebony, horn, ivory, and marquetry of stained and natural woods

72 x 110.5 x 73.6 cm (2 ft. 4³⁄₈ in. x 3 ft. 7¹⁄₂ in. x 2 ft. 5 in.)

71.DA.100

This elaborate and extremely rare piece of furniture may have been made at the Gobelins manufactory. On the other hand, the intricate marquetry of different materials could also have been the work of André-Charles Boulle (see p. 143). The wood marquetry flowers on the top of the table are very naturalistic and can readily be identified.

EWER

(Ewer) Chinese, Kangxi, 1622-1722; (mounts) French, Paris, ca. 1700-1710

Enameled porcelain; gilt bronze mounts

46.1 x 35.2 x 13.8 cm (1 ft. 6¹⁄₈ in. x 1 ft. 1⁷⁄₈ in. x 5³⁄₈ in.)

82.DI.3

This ewer is an early example of the Parisian fashion for fitting Oriental porcelain with gilt bronze mounts. Throughout the late seventeenth and eighteenth centuries the French had a passion for objects from the East but were not content with the original simple lines and elegant proportions. They preferred adding gilt bronze or silver mounts, in keeping with the luxurious tastes of the nobility.

TAPESTRY
French, Gobelins, 1715/16
Wool and silk
347 x 267 cm (11 ft. 4½ in. x 8 ft. 9¼ in.)
83.DD.20

Known as a *Char de Triomphe*, or Triumphal Chariot, this tapestry was woven
by the Gobelins manufactory after a cartoon by the painter Baudrain Yvart *père*
that was based on a design by Charles Le Brun. Called a *portière*, the tapestry
served as a decorative hanging over a doorway to block drafts. It bears the arms
of Louis XIV as king of France and Navarre. The armorial shield is surrounded
by the collars of the orders of *Saint-Esprit* and *Saint-Michèle* and is surmounted
by the head of Apollo, a symbol of the Sun King.

This tapestry was one of a series of sixty-six woven between 1662 and 1724
for use solely in the royal residences. A part of the original backing has survived
and bears a number which corresponds to the royal inventory; it records that
the tapestry was one of four delivered on October 27, 1717.

LIDDED BOWL

(Porcelain) Japanese, Imari, ca. 1700; (mounts) French, Paris, ca. 1717–1722
Hard-paste porcelain; colored enamel decoration; gilding; silver mounts
27.9 x 34 x diam. 27.5 cm (11 in. x 1 ft. 1⅜ in. x 10⅞ in.)
79.DI.123.a–b

The bluish white color of Japanese porcelain was better suited to mounts of silver than it was to gilt bronze, such as those on a ewer of similar date (see p. 146). The lid of this bowl was created by joining an inverted plate and a small lid of similar decoration. Such assemblages are not uncommon and are a mark of the inventiveness of eighteenth-century French craftsmen, many of whom remain anonymous. The silver mounts do not bear any date marks, but they can be dated stylistically to the early decades of the eighteenth century. It was during these years that nearly all Imari porcelain mounted with silver was produced.

MODEL FOR A MANTEL CLOCK
French, Paris, ca. 1700
Terracotta; enameled metal plaques
78.7 x 52.1 x 24.2 cm (2 ft. 7 in. x 1 ft. 8½ in. x 9½ in.)
72.DB.52

It is remarkable that this full-sized terracotta model for a clock has survived in such a good state of preservation. It was often the custom in the eighteenth century for a model to be ordered from a cabinetmaker for approval before the finished object was made. All of the very few such models that survive today date from the late eighteenth century. No clock of this model, which features the rape of Persephone by Pluto below the dial, seems to exist. It is possible that the model was made by one of the royal craftsmen such as the great André-Charles Boulle (see p. 150) for the approval of Louis XIV.

PEDESTAL CLOCK
Attributed to André-Charles Boulle;
movement made by Julien Le Roy
French, Paris, ca. 1715-1720
Oak veneered with tortoiseshell,
ebony, and brass; gilt bronze mounts;
enameled metal plaques
284.5 x 69.5 x 33 cm (9 ft. 4 in. x
2 ft. 3³/₈ in. x 1 ft. 1 in.)
74.DB.1

The case and pedestal of this clock
are attributed to Boulle and, typical of
his work, are entirely veneered with
tortoiseshell. The movement with
its unusual oval face is by Julien
Le Roy, who was the most eminent
clockmaker of his day. The four figures flanking the case represent the
continents of Africa, Europe, Asia,
and the Americas, while the circular
medallion set on the front of the pedestal shows Hercules relieving Atlas
of the weight of the world.

ONE OF A PAIR OF SCREENS
French, Savonnerie, 1714-1740
Wood and linen
273.6 x 193.2 cm (8 ft. 11³/₄ in. x 6 ft. 4¹/₈ in.)
83.DD.260.1-.2

With its pair, this screen of knotted wool pile was made exclusively for use in
the royal residences by the Savonnerie manufactory, which also produced carpets. Eight different designs of screens were produced, some of which are
after cartoons by Jean-Baptiste Belin de Fontenay and Alexandre-François
Desportes. The Getty model was the largest and most elaborate. Known as
paravents, such screens would have been placed to block drafts. When not in
use, the screens would have remained folded in a corner. The Museum's screens
are virtually unfaded and show the brilliant colors of the dyed wools used
at Savonnerie.

COMMODE

Made by Etienne Doirat
French, Paris, ca. 1725–1730
Oak and pine veneered with kingwood; gilt bronze mounts; marble top
86.4 x 168.9 x 71.7 cm (2 ft. 10 in. x 5 ft. 6½ in. x 2 ft. 4¼ in.)
72.DA.66

Etienne Doirat, whose name is stamped on this commode, was a French craftsman who often worked for the German market. Since the Parisian guild of *men-
uisiers-ébénistes* only instigated a rule in 1751 that all works be stamped with the
maker's name, it is unusual to find a piece of furniture stamped at this early date.

This commode may well have been intended for a German patron who
would have liked its large scale, its exaggerated *bombé* shape, and the profusion
of mounts. The lower drawer was provided with a small wheel, located at the
front in the center, to support its weight and to facilitate its opening.

SET OF FIVE VASES

German, Meissen, ca. 1730
Hard-paste porcelain; colored enamel
decoration; gilding
(Open vases) 27.6 x 17.8 cm (10⁷/₈
x 7 in.); (smaller lidded vases) 32.2 x
19.4 cm (1 ft. ¹¹/₁₆ in. x 7⁵/₈ in.); (larger
lidded vase) 37.3 x 24.1 cm (1 ft. 2¹¹/₁₆
in. x 9¹/₂ in.)
83.DE.334.1–.5

These vases were made at Meissen,
near Dresden, the first European porcelain manufactory to produce real
porcelain in imitation of Oriental
wares. They are each marked with the
AR monogram of Augustus the
Strong, Elector of Saxony, who was
the founder of the manufactory, and
are painted with a total of seventy-
two chinoiserie scenes, showing a
European idea of Chinese people and
customs. Large sets of vases such as
these have often become separated or
damaged over time, making this
group a rare survival.

COMMODE

Made by Charles Cressent
French, Paris, ca. 1735
Pine veneered with *bois satiné* and amaranth; gilt bronze mounts; marble top
90.2 x 136.5 x 64.8 cm (2 ft. 11¹/₂ in. x 4 ft. 5³/₄ in. x 2 ft. 1¹/₂ in.)
70.DA.82

The commode was made by Charles Cressent, a cabinetmaker who also forged
and gilded his own mounts. This practice of casting bronze in his workshop
transgressed the strict rules of the Parisian guild of *fondeurs-doreurs*, and Cressent was often fined for his infringement. In order to pay these fines, he held
sales of his stock and wrote the descriptive catalogues himself. The catalogue to
the sale of 1756 survives, and this commode is entered as number 132.

SIDE TABLE
French, Paris, ca. 1730
Carved and gilded wood; marble top
89.3 x 170.2 x 81.3 cm (2 ft. 11 in. x 5 ft. 7 in. x 2 ft. 8 in.)
79.DA.68

This table is intricately carved with lions' heads, dragons, serpents, and chimerae, or composite mythological beasts. While the carving is deep and pierced in many areas, the table has remarkable strength and is well able to support its heavy marble top. It was originally part of a set including two smaller side tables; they would have stood in a large *salon* fitted with paneled walls carved with similar elements. It is possible that chairs, a settee, and a fire screen, all similarly carved, once completed the furnishings of the room.

WALL CLOCK
Movement made by Charles Voisin
French, Paris and Chantilly, ca. 1740
Soft-paste porcelain; gilt bronze mounts; enameled metal dial
74.9 x 35.6 x 11.1 cm (2 ft. 5½ in. x 1 ft. 2 in. x 4⅜ in.)
81.DB.81

The case of this Rococo clock was made of soft-paste porcelain at the Chantilly manufactory, which was established in 1725 by the prince de Condé. The prince was a great collector of Japanese porcelain, and initially the Chantilly manufactory produced wares in the Japanese style. This clock may have been intended to hang over a bed and is fitted with a repeating mechanism; the pull of a string makes it strike the time.

ONE OF A PAIR OF COMMODES

Attributed to Joachim Dietrich

German, Munich, ca. 1745

Painted and gilded pine; gilt bronze mounts; marble top

83.2 x 126.4 x 61.9 cm (2 ft. 8³/₄ in. x 4 ft. 1³/₄ in. x 2 ft. ³/₈ in.)

72.DA.63.1-.2

The design of this ornately carved German commode and its pair was influenced by the engravings of François de Cuvilliés, architect for the Elector of Bavaria and one of the leading interpreters of the Rococo style. The carved side panels specifically follow an engraving by Cuvilliés in one of almost a hundred books of ornamental design published between 1738 and 1756.

ONE OF A SET OF TWO ARMCHAIRS AND TWO SIDE CHAIRS

French, Paris, ca. 1735-1740

Carved, gessoed, and gilded beechwood; modern silk upholstery

110.5 x 76.6 x 83.7 cm (3 ft. 7¹/₂ in. x 2 ft. 6¹/₈ in. x 2 ft. 8⁷/₈ in.)

82.DA.95.1-.4

This early Rococo chair belonged to a set; two additional armchairs are known to exist. The chairs are not stamped with the name of their maker since they predate the guild regulations requiring this (see p. 152). The upholstered seat, back, and arm cushions were designed so that they could be removed and re-covered according to the season of the year.

ONE OF A PAIR OF TUREENS AND STANDS
Made by Thomas Germain
French, Paris, 1726-1728
Silver
(Tureen) 17.4 x 47 x 25.4 cm (6⁷/₈ in. x 1 ft. 6¹/₂ in. x 10 in.); (stand) 3.7 x
57 x 40.6 cm (1⁷/₁₆ in. x 1 ft. 10⁷/₁₆ in. x 1 ft. 4 in.)
82.DG.12.1-.2

This large tureen and stand and its pair are marked for the years 1726 and 1728
and were made by the silversmith Thomas Germain. Germain was the finest
craftsman of his time, and he worked for the courts of France, Portugal, Brazil,
Spain, and Naples. The stands are engraved with the name of his son, François-
Thomas Germain, and it seems likely that he bought back the tureens from one
of his father's clients, had them engraved with the arms of the Portuguese
ambassador Melo e Castro, and sold them to Castro in 1764.

Tureens of the same model, without lids, appear filled with fruit in two
still life paintings by Alexandre-François Desportes. One, dated 1733, is
in the Nationalmuseum, Stockholm; the other, dated 1740, is in a European
private collection.

COMMODE

Made by Jean-Pierre Latz
French, Paris, ca. 1745-1750
Oak veneered with *bois satiné*; gilt bronze mounts; marble top
87.7 x 151.5 x 65 cm (2 ft. 10½ in. x 4 ft. 11⅝ in. x 2 ft. 2⅝ in.)
83.DA.356

Although this commode is not stamped with a cabinetmaker's name, it can be firmly attributed to Latz since his stamp is found on a commode of precisely the same design now in the Palazzo Quirinale, Rome. That commode was taken to Italy in 1753 by Louise-Elisabeth, a daughter of Louis XV, who had married Philip, Duke of Parma, son of Philip V of Spain (r. 1700-1724, 1724-1746).

CARTONNIER WITH *SERRE-PAPIER* AND CLOCK

Made by Bernard van Risenburgh; clock movement made by Etienne Le Noir
French, Paris, ca. 1745-1749
Oak veneered with ebonized wood and painted with *vernis Martin*; gilt bronze mounts; enameled metal dial; painted bronze figures
192 x 103 x 41 cm (6 ft. 3⅝ in. x 3 ft. 4⁹⁄₁₆ in. x 1 ft. 4⅛ in.)
83.DA.280

The piece is stamped B.V.R.B. for the cabinetmaker Bernard van Risenburgh. The pigeonholes in the central section and the narrow cupboards at the bottom sides were intended to contain papers. The black and gold decoration is of *vernis Martin*, a French imitation of Oriental lacquer named after the Martin brothers who invented it. In the Rococo period the use of Oriental lacquer panels to decorate expensive furniture was popular. Sometimes, however, the exotic lacquer was expensive for the client or difficult to obtain, so Parisian craftsmen learned to imitate it.

BUST OF LOUIS XV OF FRANCE

French, Mennecy, ca. 1750-1755
Soft-paste porcelain
43.2 x 24.5 x 14.5 cm (1 ft. 5 in. x
9⁹/₁₆ in. x 5¹¹/₁₆ in.)
84.DE.46

In 1734 the duc de Villeroy established
a soft-paste porcelain manufactory,
which after 1748 was located at
Mennecy. Because of the difficulties
of firing large pieces of porcelain
in the kilns, this bust of the king was
made in two pieces, joined above the
crown on the plinth. The plinth is
decorated with an asymmetrical
Rococo cartouche (enclosing the
French royal coat of arms) and with
military trophies.

DOUBLE DESK

Made by Bernard van Risenburgh
French, Paris, ca. 1750
Oak veneered with tulipwood and kingwood; gilt bronze mounts
107.8 x 158.7 x 84.7 cm (3 ft. 6½ in. x 5 ft. 2½ in. x 2 ft. 9⅜ in.)
70.DA.87

The form of this massive double desk, stamped B.V.R.B. (see p. 159), is unique.
Flaps let down on both sides to form writing surfaces, revealing pigeonholes
and small drawers. The desk was bought in Paris by the Duchess of Hamilton in
the 1760's and passed by inheritance through her second marriage to the Duke
of Argyll until it was acquired by J. Paul Getty in the 1950's.

ONE OF A SET OF FOUR WALL LIGHTS
Attributed to Jacques Caffiéri
French, Paris, ca. 1750
Gilt bronze
94 x 57.8 x 34 cm (3 ft. 1 in. x 1 ft.
10¾ in. x 1 ft. 1⅜ in.)
84.DF.41.1-.4

This Rococo wall light incorporates acanthus leaves, flowers, and pierced shellwork in its design. The set would have been hung at the sides of mirrors whose carved wood frames would have continued the design. The wall lights belonged to the royal house of Parma and are stamped with inventory marks of the Palazzo di Colorno, the court of Parma's summer residence.

COMMODE
Attributed to Joseph Baumhauer
French, Paris, ca. 1750
Oak set with Japanese lacquer and painted with *vernis Martin*; gilt bronze mounts; marble top
88.3 x 146.1 x 62.6 cm (2 ft. 10¾ in. x 4 ft. 9½ in. x 2 ft. ⅝ in.)
55.DA.2

The front and sides of this commode are set with panels of Japanese lacquer; the seams are hidden under the gilt bronze mounts. The remaining surfaces are painted in imitation of *nashiji*, a clear lacquer sprinkled with gold. This commode bears the label of the eighteenth-century furniture dealer Charles Darnault.

ONE OF A PAIR OF COMMODES

Made by Bernard van Risenburgh
French, Paris, ca. 1750
Oak veneered with tulipwood, kingwood, and amaranth; gilt bronze mounts;
marble top
87.3 x 101.9 x 55.8 cm (2 ft. 10⅜ in. x 3 ft. 4⅛ in. x 1 ft. 10 in.)
71.DA.96.1-.2

This commode and its pair are both stamped B.V.R.B. (see p. 159) and are reputed
to have been made for the Elector of Saxony, Frederick Augustus III of Poland.
They once stood in his hunting lodge, Schloss Moritzburg, together with three
larger commodes and a pair of corner cupboards. French furniture was much
admired by the various nobles and monarchs of the Continent, and, as is seen by
the robust form of this commode, the Parisian cabinetmakers often altered their
usual restrained style to suit foreign taste.

CORNER CUPBOARD

Made by Jacques Dubois; clock movement made by Etienne Le Noir
French, Paris, ca. 1755
Oak veneered with *bois satiné*, tulipwood, and rosewood; enameled metal; gilt
bronze mounts
289.5 x 129.5 x 72 cm (9 ft. 6 in. x 4 ft. 3 in. x 2 ft. 4½ in.)
79.DA.66

This cupboard stamped *I. Dubois* was made for Count Jan Clemens Branicki,
then head of the Polish army. It was delivered to him in Warsaw circa 1752, and
an inventory shows that it stood in a grand *salon* as a pendant to a large stove. Of
unique form, the cupboard is based on a print of a drawing by the great Rococo
ornamentalist Nicolas Pineau.

ONE OF A PAIR OF CABINETS

Made by Bernard van Risenburgh
French, Paris, ca. 1750–1755
Oak veneered with *bois satiné*, king-wood, and cherry; gilt bronze mounts
149 x 101 x 48.3 cm (4 ft. 10⅝ in. x
3 ft. 3¼ in. x 1 ft. 7 in.)
84.DA.24.1–.2

Stamped B.V.R.B. (see p. 159), this low cabinet and its pair are of unique form and were probably used to hold small objets d'art such as porcelains and bronzes. The cabinets are too deep to use for books. A shallow slide, situated beneath the wire-fronted upper doors, may be pulled out and may have been used by the owner while rearranging and studying his collection.

ONE OF A SET OF FOUR WALL LIGHTS

Made by François-Thomas Germain
French, Paris, 1756
Gilt bronze
99.6 x 63.2 x 41 cm (3 ft. 3¼ in. x
2 ft. ⅞ in. x 1 ft. 4⅛ in.)
81.DF.96.1–.4

Signed by François-Thomas Germain (see p. 157), these large, late Rococo wall lights were finished with an unusually high degree of attention to their casting, chasing, and gilding. It is rare for a silversmith to have worked in bronze. The lights were made for the duc d'Orléans and hung in the Palais Royal in Paris. Later in the eighteenth century they were bought by the Crown and hung in rooms used by Queen Marie-Antoinette in the chateau of Compiègne.

BASKET
French, Sèvres, 1756
Soft-paste porcelain; green ground color; gilding
22 x 20.1 x 18 cm (8⅝ x 7⅞ x 7⅛ in.)
82.DE.92

The "D" on the bottom of this basket indicates that it was made in 1756, the year the French royal porcelain manufactory moved from Vincennes to a newly built factory at Sèvres, a village on the Seine near Paris. The piece also bears the incised mark *PZ* for the modeler who cut the intricately pierced walls and made the Rococo ribbons entwining the handle. The green ground color with which this basket is painted was first developed in 1756, so this is an early example of its use.

The piece has an unusual shape. It, or one very similar to it, is described in the 1757 records of the manufactory as having been presented as a gift to François Boucher, the court painter who supplied many designs to the Sèvres manufactory.

WRITING AND TOILET TABLE

Made by Jean-François Oeben
French, Paris, ca. 1750–1755
Oak veneered with burl ash, holly, tulipwood, and other stained and natural exotic woods; gilt bronze mounts
71.1 x 80 x 42.8 cm (2 ft. 4 in. x 2 ft. 7½ in. x 1 ft. 4⅞ in.)
71.DA.103

The top of this table of multiple uses slides back, and a drawer unit can be pulled forward, revealing another sliding top concealing compartments lined with blue watered silk. These elaborate mechanisms and the fine floral and trellised marquetry decorating it are trademarks of the table's maker, royal *ébéniste* Jean-François Oeben. Toilet pots and writing materials would have been kept in this table and its surfaces used for writing. The table may have been owned by Madame de Pompadour, the mistress of Louis XV, who is shown in a contemporary painting by François Guérin (location unknown) with this table or one just like it.

LIDDED POTPOURRI VASE

French, Sèvres, ca. 1760
Enameled and gilded soft-paste porcelain
37.5 x 34.8 x 17.4 cm (1 ft. 2³/4 in. x 1 ft. 1¹¹/16 in. x 6¹³/16 in.)
75.DE.11

This *vase vaisseau à mât*, or boat-shaped vase, was designed to contain scented potpourri—dried flower petals and herbs—and its lid is pierced to allow the scent to permeate the air. The painted genre scene on the front is set into a ground of pink and green. The gold fleurs-de-lis on the pennant draped around the "mast" suggest royal ownership. This soft-paste porcelain vase is one of the most rare and elaborate of Rococo models produced in the French royal porcelain manufactory at Sèvres. Such vases were intended to be sold with others of various shapes to form a matching set, or *garniture* (see p. 153).

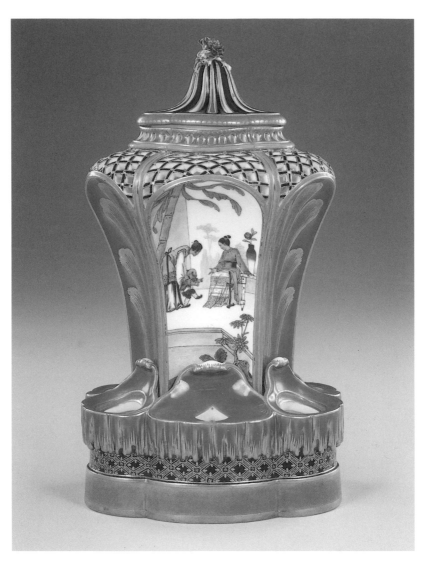

ONE OF A PAIR OF VASES
French, Sèvres, ca. 1760
Enameled and gilded soft-paste porcelain
29.8 x 16.5 x 14.6 cm (11³/₄ x 6¹/₂ x 5³/₄ in.)
78.DE.358.1-.2

The lower sections of this fountain-shaped Rococo vase and its pair were
designed to hold small flowering bulbs, while the tall central section was
intended to hold potpourri, the scent of which would emanate through the
pierced trellis at the top. Such vases would have formed a *garniture* with others
of various shapes (see pp. 153, 167). The chinoiserie scene is rare on Sèvres porcelain, and it is even more rare to find three ground colors (pink, green, and
dark blue) on one piece. Each color required a separate firing of the fragile porcelain. From archival records it is known that these vases come from a set purchased by Madame de Pompadour, mistress of Louis XV, from the Sèvres
manufactory in 1760.

MANTEL CLOCK

Case attributed to Etienne
Martincourt; movement made by
Charles Le Roy
French, Paris, ca. 1765
Gilt bronze; enameled metal
71.1 x 59.3 x 33.3 cm (2 ft. 4 in. x 1 ft.
11³/₈ in. x 1 ft. 1¹/₈ in.)
73.DB.78

Known from documents to have
belonged to Louis XVI (r. 1774-1792),
this clock is a remarkable work of
casting, since details like the rosettes
in the trellis were cast together with
the elements they decorate. The usual
practice was to cast all of these pieces
separately. Although the clock, which
came from the Palais des Tuileries, does not bear the name of its maker, a drawing for it by the *bronzier* Etienne Martincourt has recently been discovered. The
female figures flanking the urn represent Astronomy and Geography, respectively.

LIDDED BOWL ON STAND

Painted by Pierre-Antoine Méreaud *père*
French, Sèvres, 1764
Soft-paste porcelain; colored enamel decoration; gilding
12.7 x 19.7 x 21.1 cm (5 x 7³/₄ x 8⁵/₁₆ in.)
78.DE.65

Decorated in the restrained transitional style of the 1760's, when the Rococo
was giving way to the newly fashionable Neoclassical taste, this lidded bowl is
painted with the monogram and coat of arms of the eighth daughter of King
Louis XV of France, Madame Louise (see p. 173). The porcelain is marked with
the painter's mark of Méreaud *père* and the date letter "L" for 1764, the year
Madame Louise is recorded as having bought it.

ONE OF A PAIR OF VASES

French, Paris, or Italian(?), ca.
1765–1770
Porphyry; gilt bronze mounts
38.7 x 41 x 27.7 cm (1 ft. 3¼ in. x 1 ft.
4⅛ in. x 10⅞ in.)
83.DJ.16.1–.2

The simple gilt bronze mounts of
these hard stone vases, the porphyry
bowls of which were certainly cut in
Italy, exhibit bold elements typical of
early Neoclassical design—a plain
base, large drapery swag, and snake
and lion motifs. An engraving for the
composition has survived, dated 1764,
by the French architect and ornamentalist Ennemond-Alexandre Petitot,
who worked for the court of Parma
and introduced the newly emerging
Neoclassical style there.

ONE OF A PAIR OF CORNER CUPBOARDS

Made by Pierre Garnier
French, Paris, ca. 1765
Oak veneered with ebony, tulipwood,
and amaranth; gilt bronze mounts;
marble top
135.2 x 61 x 41.9 cm (4 ft. 5¼ in. x
2 ft. x 1 ft. 4½ in.)
81.DA.82.1–.2

Executed in the architectonic early
Neoclassical style, this corner cupboard and its pair take the form of
large, tapering ebony pedestals
applied to rectangles and are sparingly
decorated with classical motifs such as
laurel swags and fluting. Their maker,
Pierre Garnier, was patronized by the
marquis de Marigny (brother of
Madame de Pompadour), a well-
known champion of the new style. It
is probable that these cupboards were
made as stands for a pair of busts.

CABINET
Made by Joseph or Gaspard-Joseph Baumhauer
French, Paris, ca. 1765
Oak veneered with ebony and amaranth; gilt bronze mounts; Japanese lacquer panels; jasper top
89.6 x 120.2 x 58.6 cm (2 ft. 11¼ in. x 3 ft. 11⅜ in. x 1 ft. 11⅛ in.)
79.DA.58

The design of this early Neoclassical cabinet is severely architectonic and includes such elements as fluted, canted pilasters and Ionic capitals. Although simple in appearance, it is made from rare and expensive materials. The *kijimakie* panels, of lacquer sanded so that the grain of the wood shows, are of very fine quality and of late seventeenth-century date. A semiprecious hard stone, yellow ᐧ jasper, was used for the top instead of less expensive marble.

The cabinet is stamped JOSEPH, the mark of the cabinetmaker Joseph Baumhauer. It is likely that he worked almost entirely in the Rococo style and that this piece was in fact made by his son Gaspard-Joseph, who used his father's stamp, as was allowed by the cabinetmakers' guild.

ONE OF A SET OF FOUR TAPESTRIES
French, Gobelins, 1772/73
Wool and silk
371 x 421 cm (12 ft. 2 in. x 13 ft. 9³/₄ in.)
82.DD.66-.69

Entitled *The Arrival of Sancho on the Island of Barataria*, this tapestry is from a set of four depicting various scenes from Cervantes' *Don Quixote* that was woven at the Gobelins manufactory. They make up one of many sets woven between 1763 and 1787 after cartoons by the painter Charles Coypel. The designs of the elaborate frames and surrounds were altered periodically as styles changed. Such tapestries were often presented by the French king to royalty and nobility from other countries in Europe. This set was given by Louis XVI to the Duke and Duchess of Saxe-Teschen, who were traveling in France in 1786 (the duchess was the sister of Marie-Antoinette).

A number of examples from the *Don Quixote* series exist, but the Museum's tapestries are unusual in that the colors remain relatively unfaded and retain many of the softer hues now lost on other examples.

COMMODE

Made by Gilles Joubert
French, Paris, 1769
Oak veneered with kingwood, tulipwood, holly or boxwood, and ebony; gilt bronze mounts; marble top
93 x 181 x 67.3 cm (3 ft. ⅝ in. x 5 ft. 11¼ in. x 2 ft. 2½ in.)
55.DA.5

This commode and its pair (location unknown) were delivered in 1769 to Versailles for use in the bed chamber of Madame Louise (see p. 169). It is inscribed on the back with the number 2556, identifying it in the royal inventories. Since its maker, Gilles Joubert, was eighty years old when this piece was commissioned, it is probable that he oversaw its execution by his assistants. Joubert, best known for his Rococo work, ventured to design this commode in the newly fashionable Neoclassical style.

ONE OF A SET OF SIX WALL LIGHTS

Made by Philippe Caffiéri
French, Paris, ca. 1765-1770
Gilt bronze
64.8 x 41.9 x 31.1 cm (2 ft. 1½ in. x 1 ft. 4½ in. x 1 ft. ¼ in.)
78.DF.263.1-.4; 82.DF.35.1-.2

Signed gilt bronze objects like this one are rare since the craftsmen who made them only occasionally put their names on their work. This light is further documented by the recent discovery of a drawing signed by Philippe Caffiéri and depicting the same model. Such lights would have occupied a large *salon* fitted with three or four mirrors flanked on either side with wall lights attached to the mirror frame.

ONE OF A SET OF FOUR ARMCHAIRS AND ONE SETTEE

Made by Jean-Baptiste Tilliard *fils*
French, Paris, ca. 1770-1775
Carved and gilded beech; modern silk velvet upholstery
101.6 x 73.6 x 74.9 cm (3 ft. 3 in. x 2 ft. 5 in. x 2 ft. 5½ in.)
78.DA.99.1-.5

This armchair originally belonged to a large suite of seating furniture (another pair of chairs from the set is in the Cleveland Museum of Art). The design of the suite suggests that it was made to furnish a *grand salon*. The carving of the Neoclassical decorative elements—column-like legs, acanthus leaves, and egg-and-dart border—is extremely fine, although the frames of the pieces are massive.

WRITING TABLE

Made by Martin Carlin
French, Paris and Sèvres, ca. 1778
Oak veneered with tulipwood; gilt bronze mounts; enameled and gilded soft-paste porcelain plaques; modern leather top
77.5 x 131.2 x 62 cm (2 ft. 6½ in. x 4 ft. 3⅝ in. x 2 ft. ⅜ in.)
83.DA.385

Fourteen variously shaped plaques of soft-paste Sèvres porcelain with turquoise blue ground color were used to decorate the frieze of this Neoclassical table, which bears the paper trade label of the Parisian furniture dealer Dominique Daguerre, who sold it in the 1780's. This is the only known large writing table of this form made with such expensive plaques. The table was bought in Paris in 1784 by the future czarina of Russia, Maria Feodorovna, who took it back to the palace of Pavlovsk, outside Saint Petersburg (modern Leningrad).

SECRETAIRE
Made by Martin Carlin
French, Paris and Sèvres, ca. 1776–1777
Oak veneered with tulipwood, amaranth, and satinwood; soft-paste porcelain plaques; enameled metal; gilt bronze mounts; marble top
107.9 x 101 x 35.5 cm (3 ft. 6¼ in. x 3 ft. 3¾ in. x 1 ft. 2 in.)
81.DA.80

The upright *secrétaire*, a type of writing desk, came into fashion toward the middle of the eighteenth century. The fall front of this example lowers to form a writing surface, revealing drawers and pigeonholes. This Neoclassical *secrétaire* is decorated with specially made flower-painted Sèvres porcelain plaques (see opposite), an expensive fashion introduced by the *marchands-merciers* in the 1770's. Its unusually small size suggests that the desk was made for a bedroom.

ROLL-TOP DESK
Made by David Roentgen
German, Neuwied-am-Rhein, ca. 1785
Veneered with mahogany; gilt bronze mounts
168.3 x 155.9 x 89.3 cm (5 ft. 6¼ in. x 5 ft. 1⅜ in. x 2 ft. 11½ in.)
72.DA.47

Made in the Neoclassical style, this large desk includes a bronze plaque on the front attributed to Pierre Gouthière. When the writing surface is pulled out, a mechanism automatically withdraws the solid roll top back into the carcass, displaying the drawers and pigeonholes inside the desk. It is also fitted with both a reading-stand and a writing-surface unit, which could be used by a person standing at the closed desk. This unit is concealed, folded, behind the gilt bronze plaque; it projects forward when the weight-driven mechanism is activated by the turn of a key. The German cabinetmaker Roentgen specialized in furniture with such elaborate mechanical fittings.

STANDING VASE
(Mounts) attributed to Pierre-Philippe Thomire
(Porcelain) Chinese, ca. 1750; (mounts) French, Paris, ca. 1785
Hard-paste porcelain; colored enamel decoration; gilt bronze mounts; marble
80.7 x 56.5 cm (2 ft. 7¾ in. x 1 ft. 10¼ in.)
70.DI.115

It is possible that this large standing vase served as a jardiniere which might
have been placed on a table or stand. Another vase of identical form is in the
British Royal Collection; it was purchased by the Prince Regent (later George
IV [r. 1820-1830]) from Thomire et Cie., the company of the famous *bronzier*
Pierre-Philippe Thomire. The mounts on this vase are therefore attributed to him.

This vase was reputedly bought by Princess Isabella Lubomirska, cousin of
King Stanislas of Poland (r. 1704-1709, 1733-1735) and friend of Queen Marie-
Antoinette, at the dispersal of the French royal collection after the Revolution.

WINE BOTTLE COOLER
French, Sèvres, ca. 1790
Enameled and gilded soft-paste porcelain
18.9 x 25.8 cm (7⁷/₁₆ in. x 10³/₁₆ in.)
82.DE.5

This wine-bottle cooler is painted with a dark blue ground color and two elaborate scenes of mythological subjects surrounded by carefully tooled gilding. The scene illustrated, painted by Charles-Eloi Asselin, shows Hercules performing one of his twelve labors: capturing the man-eating horses of Diomedes. The cooler comes from one of the most important dinner services produced at Sèvres in the eighteenth century, which was ordered by Louis XVI in 1783 but not completed before his execution in 1793. The king's death marked the end of production of the costly service, of which 197 pieces had been completed. The partial service was dispersed at the time of the French Revolution. A major portion was acquired by the Prince Regent (later George IV) and can be seen today at Windsor Castle.

CHANDELIER
Made by André Galle
French, Paris, ca. 1818–1819
Gilt bronze; enameled metal; glass
129.5 x 96.5 cm (4 ft. 3 in. x 3 ft. 2 in.)
73.DH.76

The large blue enameled globe at the center of this chandelier is painted with gold stars and is encircled by a gilt bronze band with the signs of the zodiac in relief. There are eighteen candle holders, all decorated with motifs popular in the Empire period. An 1820 description survives of a chandelier of this type, written by its maker, a *bronzier* named André Galle, in which he says that the glass bowl at the bottom was for "small gold fish whose continuous movement [would] give agreeable recreation to the eye."

SCULPTURE AND WORKS OF ART

Introduction

The Department of Sculpture and Works of Art was established in 1984 with two goals. Its primary goal is to build a collection of European sculpture representing the period from the Middle Ages to the end of the nineteenth century. Its other main goal is to complement the Department of Decorative Arts (responsible for Northern European decorative arts from 1650 to 1900) and to build the Museum's collection of all European decorative arts from the period prior to 1650 and in Southern Europe from 1650 to 1900. The department's collection presently includes Italian Renaissance maiolica; Venetian, Spanish, and Northern glass ranging in date from the fifteenth to the seventeenth century; sculptures of the late sixteenth and seventeenth centuries by the artists Giambologna, Hendrick de Keyser, and Rombout Verhulst; a small group of eighteenth-century bronzes and portrait busts; and fine examples of Italian furniture from the sixteenth, seventeenth, and eighteenth centuries.

In coming years the department's collection will expand from this base.

"OAK-LEAF" JAR
Made by the workshop of Giunta di Tugio (?)
Italian, Florence, ca. 1431
Tin-glazed earthenware
H: 25 cm (9¾ in.)
84.DE.98

Maiolica, so called because many of the earliest examples of these ceramic works came to Italy from Spain through the Spanish port of Majorca, is porous earthenware covered with a tin or lead opaque white glaze which provides a suitable ground for painted decoration. Giunta di Tugio was the most important maiolica maker of his time in Florence. He brought great fame to the maiolica workshop of his father, which the younger di Tugio directed for nearly thirty years until his death of the plague in 1450.

Giunta di Tugio's workshop may have produced this apothecary jar since the area below the handles bears the six-pointed asterisk mark common on wares attributed to that workshop. The jar was made for the pharmacy of the Santa Maria Nuova hospital in Florence, for which the shop furnished close to a thousand pieces. The crutch painted in green on each of the two strap handles was the symbol of the hospital. The dominant motif is the leaf—possibly of the Turkey oak or grapevine—which is decoratively distributed over the jar's surface and frames the image of a running saddle-back boar.

BOWL
Italian, Venice, ca. 1500
Chalcedony glass
12.5 x diam. 19.6 cm (4¹⁵/₁₆ x 7³/₄ in.)
84.DK.660

This rare object is one of a small extant group of Renaissance bowls in chalcedony, or agate, glass, so called because of the opaque, marbled appearance which resembles natural hard stones. Chalcedony glass probably was developed as a result of the experiments of late fifteenth-century chemists and glass technicians such as the Venetian Barovier family. Highly prized for the beauty of its colors and as a curiosity, chalcedony glass is another example of the Renaissance revival of antiquity, since this type of glass was first made in Roman times.

ISTORIATO DISH

Painted by Francesco Xanto Avelli da Rovigo
Italian, Urbino, 1534
Tin-glazed earthenware
Diam. 46 cm (18 1/8 in.)
84.DE.118

Istoriato, or historiated, maiolica pieces literally depict a "story." Francesco
Xanto Avelli derived his stories from engravings, mostly from those of Marc-
antonio Raimondi after Raphael, as in the case of this dish. Avelli is one of the
very few maiolica painters of the 1530's to show the influence of contemporary
events in his work. The deep impression left by the horrors of the sack of Rome
by German mercenary troops in 1527 may well have influenced the choice of
the subject matter of this dish: the abduction of Helen by the Trojans, a theme
which appears on many maiolica dishes of the early sixteenth century. Moreover, Avelli often introduced inscriptions commenting upon events of his own
day. The inscription on the underside of this piece includes the date and artist's
signature as well as a verse describing the painted mythological scene: "This is
the shepherd [Paris] who saw the beautiful face of Helen of Greece and that
famous abduction which threw the world into confusion."

At the beginning of the sixteenth century, rimless dishes became popular
because they allowed the painter to extend his decoration over the entire surface
of the piece. This practice was particularly appropriate for *istoriato* ware such as
this dish, on which the figures are dramatically grouped in the foreground,
allowing the landscape to create subtle effects of distance.

HENDRICK DE KEYSER
Dutch, 1565–1621
A Warrior on Horseback, ca. 1610–1620
Bronze; modern wood base
H: 39.6 cm (15⅝ in.)
84.SB.90

Hendrick de Keyser was a major sculptor and one of the most important architects in Holland at the end of the sixteenth and beginning of the seventeenth centuries. In addition to his activities as an architect and designer of monumental sculpture, de Keyser produced a number of small table bronzes and played a key role in bringing this type of object to the Lowlands, figural table bronzes having been primarily an Italian and German idiom throughout the late fifteenth and sixteenth centuries. This armor-clad warrior on horseback, created as an independent work, was probably intended to represent a figure from mythology or ancient history. The Medusa head on the shield brings to mind the hero Perseus; however, rearing horse and rider groups of this type commonly depict the Roman hero Marcus Curtius. The rider sits very far back on the horse. This was done, at least in part, to move the center of gravity of the bronze over the horse's rear legs so that the group would stand balanced on the rear hooves.

ROMBOUT VERHULST
Dutch, 1624–1698
Bust of Jacob van Reygersberg, 1671
Marble
H: 63 cm (24³/₄ in.)
84.SA.743

This bust of an important Dutch government official combines the extraordinarily subtle naturalism—in the differentiation of the textures of flesh, hair, lace jabot, and armor—and the Baroque compositional devices that characterize Verhulst's work. Verhulst was particularly innovative in dealing with the formal problem of how to truncate the human figure in busts. In the portrait of Van Reygersberg, Verhulst introduced decorative curving volutes that finish off the bust and frame it; at the same time their curving forms lead the viewer's eye upward to focus on the sitter's face.

GIAMBOLOGNA (Giovanni da Bologna)
Flemish, 1529–1608
Bathing Venus, ca. 1559
Marble
H: (sculpture) 115 cm (45¹/₄ in.); (plinth) 7 cm (2³/₄ in.)
82.SA.37

Giambologna is the Italian name for the Flemish artist Jean Boulogne, who trained in his native Flanders before moving to Italy in the 1550's. He established himself in Florence under the patronage of the Medicis and became that city's greatest sculptor after the death of Michelangelo in 1564.

An early work by the artist, the *Bathing Venus* depicts a nude woman seated on a truncated column, holding up an ointment jar and drying her left foot. The deliberately complex counterspiral pose is one of the earliest examples of the so-called *figura serpentinata*, which was to typify much late sixteenth-century Mannerist sculpture. Both this ambitious pose and the sensuous rendering of the flesh attest to Giambologna's virtuosity as a marble sculptor. The Getty statue was documented in Sweden in the 1680's, where it was described as Bathsheba—who is often portrayed bathing while being watched by King David—thus giving this naked figure the guise of biblical respectability.

Only about a dozen marble sculptures by Giambologna are known. The *Bathing Venus* is the first such sculpture by this artist to be in an American collection and the first major example of post-antique sculpture acquired by the Museum.

SIDE TABLE
Italian, Rome, ca. 1720
Gessoed and gilded limewood; modern top
93.9 x 190.5 x 96.5 cm (47 x 75 x 38 in.)
82.DA.8

This massive table, carved with masks and heads, can be completely disassembled for easy transport, an unusual feature for an object of this size, which would have formed part of an architectural setting in one of the grander Roman palazzos. Its pair is in the Palazzo Barberini, but it is not known if that table is in its original setting. Made for a *galleria,* the Getty table would probably have supported a large bronze sculpture or Chinese porcelain vases.

CRUCIFIX
(Corpus) French (?), ca. 1690–1700; (cross) French, ca. 1770–1775
Boxwood and oak veneered with ebony; gilt bronze mounts; brass and gilt bronze stringing
H: 124 cm (59 in.)
82.SD.138

The large and beautifully carved *Corpus Christi* dates from the late seventeenth century and was probably carved either in France or the Netherlands. The calm and idealized posture of the figure, however, indicates that it may have been loosely based on an Italian model. Roughly a century after it was carved, the figure was mounted on a fine ebony cross and base and set with gilt bronze mounts in the newly fashionable Neoclassical style. It can be surmised that the eighteenth-century owner highly prized this figure and wished to modernize it by having the sculpture mounted in a way that would reflect contemporary tastes. The snake at the base of the cross is both a symbol of immortality and a reference to the garden of Eden, signifying Christ as the second Adam. The gilt bronze medallion on the base holds a depiction of the head of the Virgin. The names of the craftsmen responsible for this fine object are not known.

ATTRIBUTED TO GIOVANNI BATTISTA FOGGINI
Bacchus and Ariadne, ca. 1690
Italian, 1622-1740
Patinated bronze
H: 40 cm (13³/₄ in.)
83.SB.333

This bronze group depicts Bacchus and Ariadne resting after the latter's rescue on the island of Naxos. Bacchus holds a bunch of grapes and a wine cup, while Ariadne is shown squeezing grapes into a ewer of wine. The group can be attributed to Giovanni Battista Foggini, who became court sculptor in Florence in 1687. A plaster model of this group was sold by his son, after the father's death, to the Ginori porcelain manufactory at Doccia, outside Florence. As a result, porcelain versions of the group exist. Pictorial compositions showing two figures interacting and composed to be read primarily from a single, frontal viewpoint are typical of early eighteenth-century Florentine bronzes.

COMMODE

Italian, Venice, ca. 1750–1760

Gilded, silvered, and painted wood; oak and pine top painted to imitate marble

81.5 x 147 x 62.5 cm (32⅛ x 57⅞ x 24⅝ in.)

83.DA.282

Most Venetian furniture of the mid–eighteenth century was painted and not veneered with wood marquetry. Similarly, gilt bronze mounts and marble tops were rarely employed. Most painted commodes are now delapidated, but this example is in a remarkably good state of preservation. Only the silvering of the raised moldings has suffered; it has oxidized, and the original bright contrast between silver and gold is mostly gone. However, the glittering effect of the strongly colored flowers against the gold ground is still effective. Such a sumptuous piece would have been made for one of the grander palaces of Venice.

PHOTOGRAPHS

Introduction

In mid-1984 the Museum established a new curatorial department
dedicated to the art of photography. The opportunity to acquire several
of the most important private collections of photographs in the world
may be compared to the establishment of the Department of Manuscripts
through the acquisition of the finest gathering of illuminated manuscripts in private hands. The Museum decided to form a photography
collection for reasons similar to those advanced in favor of collecting
manuscripts and drawings: photography is an art fundamental to its time
in which individual works of great rarity, beauty, and historical importance have been made.

Among the collections acquired in their entireties were those
of Samuel Wagstaff, Arnold Crane, Bruno Bischofberger, and
Volker Kahmen/George Heusch. The gathering of these collections,
along with other block acquisitions made at the same time, has brought
to Los Angeles the most comprehensive corpus of photographs on the
West Coast.

The photographs reproduced in this *Handbook* represent a survey
of some of the strengths of the collection, which is particularly rich in
examples dating from the early 1840's and which includes major holdings
by William Henry Fox Talbot, Louis-Jacques-Mandé Daguerre, David
Octavius Hill and Robert Adamson, Hippolyte Bayard, Sir John
Herschel, and other early practitioners who worked around Talbot in
England and Daguerre in France. The collection also includes significant
works by some of the most important photographers of the first half of
the twentieth century and is international in scope. Its guiding principal
is the belief in the supremacy of certain individual master photographers
and in the timeless importance of individual master photographs.

For conservation reasons, photographs, like manuscripts and drawings,
cannot be kept on permanent display. At the present time the collection
is available to the public by appointment in a study room located in the
J. Paul Getty Center for the History of Art and the Humanities, Santa
Monica. By mid-1986 selected photographs will be presented in rotating
exhibitions in a gallery at the Museum in Malibu.

CHARLES R. MEADE
American, 1827-1858
Portrait of Louis-Jacques-Mandé
Daguerre, 1848
Daguerreotype
16 x 12 cm (6⁵/₁₆ x 4¹³/₁₆ in.)
84.XT.953

UNIDENTIFIED
PHOTOGRAPHER
Edgar Allan Poe, late October 1848(?)
Daguerreotype
12.2 x 8.9 cm (4¹³/₁₆ x 3¹/₂ in.)
84.XT.957

For reasons that are not entirely clear, relatively few daguerreotypes of famous persons have survived from the 1840's. Daguerre himself, for example, the father of his profession, was photographed a mere handful of times. The most important of his portraits to survive were made by a stranger, the American Charles Meade. Meade was one of the most prominent daguerreian portraitists

in New York and traveled to France specifically to gain an audience with Daguerre. The Getty portrait is one of five by Meade that are known and is typical in its lighting and in the serene pose of the sitter, whose elbow rests on the table and whose hands are clasped one over the other.

The art of the daguerreotype is one in which the identity of the sitter has often come to have more importance than the name of the maker. This is particularly true in the case of Edgar Allan Poe. Four of the six times that Poe is documented to have posed for a daguerreotypist occurred within the last year of the writer's life. The Getty *Poe* was presented by him to Annie Richmond, one of two women to whom he made romantic declarations in the months following the death of his wife in early 1847. Poe, who has been described as a libertine, a drug addict, and an alcoholic, is represented here as an individual who might well have been the victim of his own unharnessed emotions.

WILLIAM HENRY FOX TALBOT
British, 1800–1877
Oak Tree, mid-1840's
Salt print from paper negative
22.5 x 18.9 cm (8⁷/₈ x 7⁷/₁₆ in.)
84.XM.893.1

Talbot's most important invention was one that is easily taken for granted today: the negative from which faithful replicas can be produced. He patented this procedure under the trade name "calotype." Talbot intended his invention to be clearly distinguished from the daguerreotype. Daguerre's procedure resulted in pictures on metal plates that could not be multiplied easily. Daguerreotypes were used almost exclusively for studio portraiture since sitters generally required but a single example, while calotypes required less fussy procedures and therefore were favored when a particular subject had an audience of more than one. Early photographers favored Talbot's process when they traveled for landscape work.

There is no known surviving early daguerreotype of a single tree. Yet trees were a favorite subject for photographers who were influenced by the aesthetic of picturesque romanticism evident in Talbot's treatment of this image.

HIPPOLYTE BAYARD
French, 1801–1887
Arrangement of Specimens, ca. 1841
(from Bayard Codex)
Direct positive print
27.7 x 21.6 cm ($10^{15}/_{16}$ x $8^{1}/_{2}$ in.)
84.XO.968

Bayard was a friend of Daguerre who recognized that the daguerreotype process was flawed: the image could not be multiplied on paper with satisfactory fidelity to the appearance of the original. Inspired by Talbot, Bayard independently devised a way to make paper photographs; however, like the daguerreotype, they were one-of-a-kind objects and could not be replicated faithfully. Bayard's elegant arrangement of plant specimens, textile fragments, and a feather is an experimental forerunner of a working method that the twentieth-century photographer Man Ray thought he invented.

WILLIAM HENRY
FOX TALBOT
British, 1800–1877
Lady Elizabeth Fielding,
August 21, 1841
(from Brewster Codex)
Calotype
18 x 11.2 cm (7¹/₁₆ x 4⁷/₁₆ in.)
84.XZ.574

DR. JOHN ADAMSON
British, 1810–1870
Mr. Thomson, ca. 1842
(from Brewster Codex)
Calotype
18.6 x 14.4 cm (7⁵/₁₆ x 5¹¹/₁₆ in.)
84.XZ.574

DAVID OCTAVIUS HILL
AND ROBERT ADAMSON
British, 1802–1870; 1821–1848
Newhaven Fisherman, 1844–1848
Calotype
20.7 x 15 cm (8¹/₁₆ x 5¹⁵/₁₆ in.)
84.XM.445.1

The first genuine flowering of photography as a means of artistic expression took place not in England or France but in Scotland, where Talbot's patent on the calotype was invalid. A circle of talented scientists, who revolved around Sir John Herschel and who included Sir David Brewster and Dr. John Adamson, succeeded in perfecting Talbot's paper negative process before he did. The lucky beneficiaries of this information, circa 1843/1844, were John Adamson's brothers, Henry and Robert. The latter went into partnership with the painter David Octavius Hill, and in 1844 established a studio to make paper negative portraits in Edinburgh. The results of this collaboration are generally accepted as the first corpus of photographs made as works of art rather than as scientific experiments, as well as being the first to surpass Talbot in richness and permanence.

The Museum is fortunate to possess a codex that is believed to have been assembled by one of the Brewster brothers, possibly Sir David himself. The importance of the Brewster Codex lies in its being the only source in which

experimental British and Scottish photographs dating from the early 1840's may be studied side by side. Thus it is possible to judge how distant Talbot was even in 1844 from the formula known to the Scots for making richly toned, permanent photographs. The image of Talbot's mother hovers like a ghost on the surface of the paper, and its pale tones are a self-evident indication of how far behind the Scots Talbot was. The Hill and Adamson calotypes, in comparison, are the rich purple-brown typical of the first photographs made after one of the Brewster brothers discovered that toning with gold chloride was the key to creating a permanent photograph.

NADAR (Gaspard-Félix Tournachon)
French, 1820–1910
Self-Portrait, ca. 1855
Salt print
20.5 x 16.9 cm (8¹¹/₁₆ x 6⅝ in.)
84.XM.436.2

Nadar turned his back on the tradition of portraiture that had been established
by the daguerreian generation. Daguerreotype portraits were generally formal
and hieratic, in contrast to the informality and naturalism that Nadar wished to
express and that are typified by this self-portrait. The word "candid," though
not in use in connection with photography in the 1850's, best describes Nadar's
point of view. He made numerous self-portraits in order to experiment with
various poses and gestures.

Nadar always posed his subjects against the same neutral background and
placed them below a skylight which cast gentle light from above and left delicate shadows under the eyes, around the nose, and in facial folds and hollows.
His ultimate goal was to create a corpus of photographs representing the most
celebrated citizens of Paris in the arts, literature, and the professions during the
Second Empire. He called this undertaking the *Panthéon Nadar*.

JULIA MARGARET CAMERON
British, 1815-1879
Hallam Tennyson, 1867
Albumen print
33.2 x 26.5 cm (13 1/6 x 10 9/16 in.)
84.XM.443.1

Julia Margaret Cameron began to photograph a decade after Nadar and took as her subjects family members, household domestics, and friends. Some of the latter were luminaries of her time, such as Sir John Herschel and Alfred Lord Tennyson. Deeply influenced by Pre-Raphaelite art, Cameron sought to dramatize and fictionalize her sitters. She experimented continuously with unconventional techniques. Here the choice of light cast from behind the sitter stresses the nose that was a Tennyson family trademark. Typical of Cameron's unconventional approach is the out-of-focus center of interest, which may have been the result of the camera's having moved slightly during the process of exposure.

ALEXANDER GARDNER
American, 1821–1882
Lincoln on the Battlefield of Antietam, Maryland, 1862
Albumen print
22 x 19.6 cm (8⅝ x 7¾ in.)
84.XM.482.1

Lincoln was the first American president to recognize the importance of photography and to make time in his busy life to be photographed on many occasions. Most of the surviving photographs of him were made in Washington, D.C., or in village studios in Illinois. Here we see the commander-in-chief conferring with Major General John McClernand and Major Allan Pinkerton, Chief of the Secret Service, in the combat zone.

The genius of this photograph lies in Gardner's ability to build a composition around the intrusive details of camp life. The tent and tent lines dominate the composition. Thus the viewer's eye is drawn as much to the fastenings on the lines as it is to the faces of the principals. Despite compositional interruptions, however, the statuesque figure of Lincoln remains the center of interest.

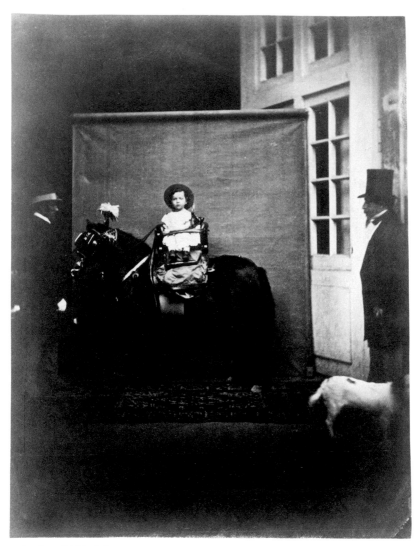

LOUIS PIERSON
French, 1818-1913
Napoleon III and the Prince Imperial, ca. 1859
Albumen photograph
20.4 x 15.6 cm (8 1/16 x 6 1/8 in.)
84.XM.705

In nineteenth-century photographs, children were generally posed seated in a chair with their heads clamped firmly in place. Photographers required studios with good natural light until the advent of the magnesium flash late in the century. Thus photographs could generally be made only during daylight hours.

This photograph no doubt was made at the emperor's command late in the day when the light came from an oblique angle, leaving deep shadows. The Oriental carpet and cloth backdrop are props intended to disguise the outdoor location. A butler whose white gloves, white shirt collar, and hatband reveal him in the shadow, holds the pony's bridle, while the emperor himself tends a small dog, whose rump and haunches dominate the foreground.

COLONEL STUART WORTLEY
British, 1832–1890
The Day is Done, and the Darkness Falls from the Wings of Night, ca. 1862
Albumen print
29.5 x 35 cm (11⅝ x 13⅞ in.)
84.XM.644.1

The light-sensitive materials in use before circa 1880 were receptive principally to blue light and hardly sensitive at all to red light. For this reason the sky in most early photographs reads as white in the print, and clouds are rarely evident. Sunrise and sunset were particularly difficult to capture because red is their principal color..

Wortley succeeded in photographing clouds at a time when few others were able to do so. The French photographer Gustave LeGray preceded him in attaining this goal but did so from a different motivation. Like Nadar (see p. 202), LeGray was interested in natural effects; Wortley, like Cameron (see p. 201), was interested in the poetic and the fictional. Here Wortley has represented a coastal town with clouds printed from a separate negative. Since his intent was literary and not technical, he added several lines of verse below the photograph to insure that his purpose was clear to all who saw it.

CARLETON E. WATKINS
American, 1829-1916
Columbia River, Oregon, 1867
Albumen print
40.5 x 52.3 cm (16^1/₁₆ x 20^{11}/₁₆ in.)
85.XM.11.2

While the Civil War was raging in the Eastern United States, Westerners, still buoyant from post-Gold Rush prosperity, continued to lead normal lives. The best Eastern contemporaries of Watkins—Gardner, O'Sullivan, and Russell—spent their time photographing aspects of the war (see p. 202), while Watkins, who ranks among the greatest American photographers of all time, had the leisure to ripen his style to full maturity between 1861 and 1868. Watkins had the gift of being able to create complex compositions from very simple motifs and the power of perception to apprehend ephemeral forces in nature that form a seamless web of formal relationships. The three key elements of this picture are the massiveness of the rock formations at either side, the transient quality of the boat loaded with boxes of enormous apples, and the delicacy of the light reflected from the water's surface.

Watkins designed photographs brilliantly to achieve a painterly interplay between surface pattern and spatial dimensions. The network of intricately connected compositional elements evident in *Columbia River, Oregon* is chiefly responsible for the picture's palpable sense of space and is typical of this concern. Watkins' photographs were used as reference sources by painters such as Thomas Hill and Albert Bierstadt.

Watkins was also an excellent technician who worked in a variety of materials. He frequently made stereographs, a type of miniature photograph that functioned for him as a sketching medium. After visualizing his subject, he would proceed to make mammoth plate negatives that yielded the presentation prints for which he was most celebrated.

THOMAS EAKINS
American, 1844–1916
Unidentified Models in Eakins'
Studio, ca. 1883
Platinum print
16.3 x 25 cm (6⅜ x 9⅞ in.)
84.XM.155.38

EDGAR DEGAS
French, 1834–1917
Seated Nude, ca. 1895
Gelatin silver print
17 x 12 cm (6¹¹/₁₆ x 4¾ in.)
84.XM.495.1

Photography was invented just when painters collectively seemed to require a
new way of seeing the world. Although many nineteenth-century painters dab-
bled in photography, very few carried their experiments far enough to produce
a significant corpus of work. Two painters who did, and who are still univer-
sally respected, were Edgar Degas and Thomas Eakins.

   Degas and Eakins became aware of photography in the early 1880's
through the serial studies of animals and humans in motion of Etienne-Jules
Marey in France and of Eadweard Muybridge in America. Degas and Eakins
both made multiple-exposure photographs that challenged contemporary
understanding of time and space. Their most memorable photographs, however, embody the traditional procedures of observing a subject closely and
of forming an attractive compositon. From beginnings on the experimental
fringe of photography, Degas and Eakins both came to use the camera as a
sketching tool to delineate effects of light, gesture, and costume.

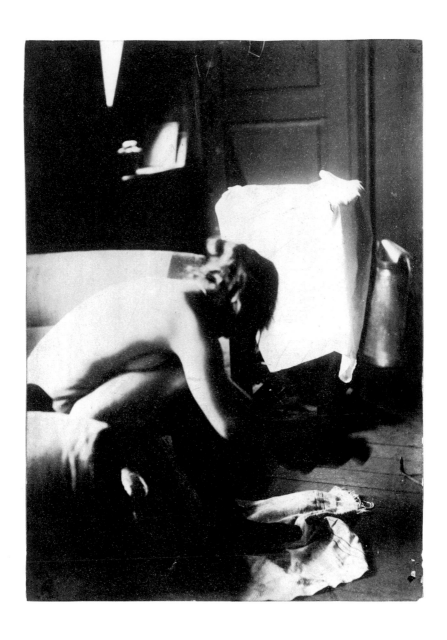

LEWIS HINE
American, 1874-1940
Self-Portrait with Newsboy, ca. 1910
Gelatin silver print
14 x 11.9 cm (5½ x 4¹¹⁄₁₆ in.)
84.XM.967.1

Included in this photograph by Lewis Hine, who has come to be admired for his selfless limning of working children in the years before child-labor laws were enacted, is an inadvertent self-portrait, a bonus bestowed along with the finely visualized principal subject. We see the shadow of a figure wearing hat and suit through which lines on the pavement intersect like a conceptual grid. The silhouette, surely that of Hine, provides items of information pertaining to the making of the photograph. In the photographer's right hand is a pneumatic bulb connected by a tube to a medium-sized, tripod-mounted plate-camera. The newsboy wears a hat advertising Coca-Cola, but he does not seem exceptional in any way. Thus the question of why Hine chose to photograph this particular boy and why he had his camera positioned at this particular corner demands consideration. It may have been less the boy's image per se than the serendipitous confluence of light and form that caught Hine's eye.

ALEXANDER RODCHENKO
Russian, 1891–1956
En Route, 1932
Gelatin silver print
18 x 12 cm (7¹/₈ x 4³/₄ in.)
84.XM.258.1

During the decade following the Russian Revolution of 1917, avant-garde experiments by important artists were briefly thought to reflect the ideals of the newly created state. Photographers experimented with both worm's-eye and bird's-eye points of view, as well as with telephoto lenses, extreme enlargements, and action-filled subjects such as the political rally represented here. This photograph functions as both art and political propaganda.

MAN RAY (Emmanuel Rudnitsky)
American, 1890–1976
Still Life composed for *Minotaure,* 1933
Three-color carbon transfer
30.7 x 23.9 cm (12¹/₁₆ x 9³/₈ in.)
84.XM.1000.6

In one way or another, all of the photographs illustrated in this *Handbook* manifest a sense of experiment, but none so overtly as this one. Man Ray has created a still life from an arrangement of found objects with one of his own black-and-white photographs, a study of a model with glass tears, also in the Getty Museum. This composition is a kind of surrealist manifesto that proves how important context is to the identity of an object. It is also an experiment in the arrangement of forms and in the photographing of different colors. Vivid blues and yellows are juxtaposed with the monochrome of the background black-and-white photograph and with the off-white of a plaster portrait bust. The print was made by means of the three-color carbon transfer process, which is the most permanent type of color photograph ever devised.

FRANCIS BRUGIERE
American, 1879-1945
Untitled (Cut Paper), ca. 1928
Gelatin silver print
35.5 x 27.9 cm (14 x 11 in.)
84.XM.469.1

Although light is the principal activating force in a photograph, it was not until the twentieth century that photographers began to recognize that light and dark areas, together with the edges produced where they met, could themselves be the successful subjects of a photograph. While the earliest photographers had created designs by placing objects directly upon light-sensitive printing paper (see p. 197), Brugière exercised a leap of the imagination by cutting designs into a sheet of artist's drawing paper and then placing the cut sheet on top of photographic paper, which recorded the variations in gray created by light passing through the sliced openings. The resulting picture was made without the intervention of camera and lens, yet it retains the dimensionality of a well-visualized bas relief.

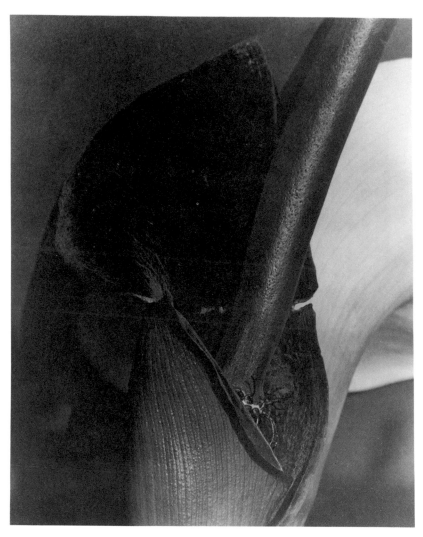

IMOGEN CUNNINGHAM
American, 1883-1976
Black and White Lily, 1928/1929
Gelatin silver print
30 x 23.4 cm (11⅝ x 9³/₁₆ in.)
84.XP.208.1

We generally have little difficulty in determining when a painting or sculpture is the product of its maker's imagination. Imagination is a more difficult concept to grasp in the art of photography and generally involves seeing familiar objects in unexpected ways. In this photograph, first shown in the 1929 exhibition *Film und Foto* in Stuttgart (catalogue number 165), Cunningham used imagination to retain a delicate balance between recognizable actuality and stylization. The print challenges our ability to decipher its subject by eliminating the white range of the tonal scale, thus blurring the edges between shapes in a way not unlike a painting made with a very broad brush.

WALKER EVANS
American, 1903–1975
Promenade Deck of the Queen Mary. Bow View, Port Side, ca. 1958
Gelatin silver print
26.4 x 26.8 cm (10³/₈ x 10¹⁷/₃₂ in.)
84.XM.488.1

Walker Evans is so often associated with photographs of Southern dirt farmers and their ramshackle habitations that this image comes as a surprise. We see here that Evans ultimately had as much in common with the formalism of Charles Sheeler as he had with the social conscience of Ben Shahn. Like paint- ers, photographers are continuously torn between form and content as the goals of expression, and they also demonstrate similar cycles of artistic growth which may, at different times, accommodate divergent stylistic premises. Evans' career as a photographer commenced shortly after his return from a European trip on a liner built about the time of the *Queen Mary*. The concern with abstract forms visible in manmade objects that manifested itself in his photographs of the 1950's actually was a revival of an interest apparent in his photographs of New York taken thirty years earlier.

AUGUST SANDER
German, 1876–1964
Frau Peter Abelen, Cologne, 1926
Gelatin silver print
22.9 x 17.4 cm (9 x 6⁷/₁₆ in.)
84.XM.498.9

BERND AND HILLA
BECHER
German, b. 1931; 1934
Cooling Tower, 1968
Gelatin silver photograph
23.9 x 17.9 cm (9³/₈ x 7¹/₁₆ in.)
84.XM.125.37

Although ambiguity is considered a great shortcoming in the written or spoken word, it is a very powerful force in the art of photography. This pair of pictures raises more questons than it answers. If one did not know the title of the Sander, one would wonder whether a male or female was represented, or whether the emotion of hate or longing was expressed on the face. Both photographs also are linked by their ambiguity as documents or works of art.

Sander's and the Bechers' work is also joined by the principle of comparability, the presentation of photographs of like subjects (people for the former, structures for the latter) that must be observed one against the other for the maker's intent to be realized. The trait shared by Sander and the Bechers is the passion of the collector: Sander "collected" the faces and physiques of human beings, while the Bechers "collect" the shapes and details of industrial artifacts. All three have understood that their subjects exist on a scale of quality and in versions that are antetypes and variants. The photographers' pleasure, and much of ours, derives from recognizing patterns of organization, formal sequences, and the internal utopia created by satisfying the instinctive human belief that order exists.